"911 AND THE ORACLE OF

WAS"

~ ~ ~

SUB: 'WASHINGTON ARCH SQUARE' THE TERRORIST
ABDUCTION, EPIPHANY & MARCH ON WALL ST.'

BY

Nicholas Conti

WWW.NickConti.com   & WWW.DOOLLEE.COM

By AWARD WINNING PLAYWRIGHT

NICHOLAS CONTI

Whose plays have been performed throughout the United States, UK, Ireland, Tasmania, Singapore etc. First Coveted Award received at Gettysburg College (PA). For "The Merry Women of Windham," It later Winning in Dublin, and which is now published with Lazy Bee Scripts UK. Also Placing was the award winning "Alessandro," at Cunneen Hackett Center, Poughkeepsie NY.

DEDICATION

TO THE LOVING SUPPORT OF MY SONS:

COLONEL GREG CONTI & FAMILY,

DANIEL CONTI & JENN AND MY

LOVE CHRIS CONTI, HER ENDURING

PATIENCE AND INSPIRATION!

NICK CONTI

<> DRAMATISTS GUILD OF AMERICA <>

ALSO BY NICK CONTI

PLAYS, BOOKS & THINGS

"The Miniscule Chronicles"& "The Legacy."

"Dickens' of a Christmas Tree," "A Dickens of a Christmas," Godmother I & Godmother I-101,

"Godmother I and the Grump That Stole Christmas," "Nicolas and Rudy," *all* @ **DramaSource.com.**

The Award Winning: "The Merry Women of Windham," Award winning "Alessandro;" "Mirror Mirror on the Wall" & Fone Home *all* @ **LazyBeeScripts.co.uk...**

"Hamalot," @ **BigDogPlays.com...** "Wenceslas," *Taming of a Bull(Y),* "Chris Carole Meet Santa," "Shades of Sylvia," "Little Miracle of Bethlehem," "The Mystery of the House of the 7 Gables," "The Little Drummer Boy;" *all* @ **Jac Publishing, on the Web and Amazon...**

"Night of the Living Cryonic Dead," @ **Meriwether Publishing (WEB). Commissioned: "The Quadricentennial Military Pageant,** City of Poughkeepsie, NY in 2009. <> "The Dragon Who Could Sing Bass," Publ. Whimsy Mag. 2004, & "Doctologists," Publ. Placebo Journal 2004 & Theater Memories, Publ. Savannah Mag. Dec. 2001. **Books & Poetry Published on Amazon and on Kindle: "Fables of the Hudson Valley Miniscules"** About the **Gnomes amongst us and in Our Valley!** ~ **" PrimeTime Rhymes" and "Jailhouse Armageddon" which concerns Breaking into a Maximum Prison & The Mafia. And the Latest addition; "The Cryacula Genesis," about Frozen Horror with a Bite!**

Acknowledgements: God, My Family, Loves, Life, Friends, Scouting USN, Travels, Theater, Radio, Music, Singing, Publishing, Playwriting. Will Shakespeare, Lord Byron, Dorothy Parker, Charles Dickens, Billy Crystal.

Alexander Hamilton & John Barrymore.

Contents:

THE PREFACE

'The WAS' is! 'The Washington Arch Square.' Nate's home, he's
a squatter!... With its bend-down watch your head entrance!
Then climb the winding staircase to Nate's Brick encapsulated
Abode, some believe to be Nate the Oracle's Doric Temple... His
reputation growing, so is his security risk!... Later on, ' Taken
Hostage' more on that later! Experiences an Epiphany,
somewhere along the line, arousing his friends in the Sunrise
Club: Nan Goodhart; Harry (Har); Mary (Mar) into becoming
seriously involved Activists. Then there's Ma: Harry's Mom, then
there are his Political friends   Mayor Ed Koach, and
Senator Hildy Brodrik Minton. Picketing & working toward
Peace, Jobs, Food, and Shelter for the Homeless, Disabled and

Vets!... Will they be successful?............... YOU GOTTA

BELIEVE !

THE ORACLE'S *** PROLOGUE OF WAS !

If you're a West Village habitué as I was you'll recognize the neighborhood at first sight. If not imagine the setting with a backdrop of The Washington Arch··· If you imagine carefully you'll see a short, old, solid Steel Door, on the Southerly side where one must be sure to lower one's head upon entering at the risk of decapitation! Be Warned! It's the surreptitious Open Sesame to Nate's, our Oracle's humble Pad. I mean it does require some effort to wander through a chilly-damp

8

stairwell in order to arrive at Nate's select but homestead⋯ Nothing fancy, lit by an odd, oversized work light when on the rare occasion a workman shows up to repair something. On the floor sprawled colorfully if not fitfully is an unholy, stained, no longer in fashion flower child's Hippie style bedroll, mournfully, uncomfortable, that takes getting used to⋯ Needless to say is heedlessly dank with spiders, ants or centipedes occasionally running through it; lending an air of lively, vitality to his bed. In the corner notice and old, dirty, apple-crate dating from when they used to be made out of sturdy wood⋯ Now follow the weird shadow that the overhead light casts leading you to an *Orange- crate*, very old but still solid with essence of oranges long since having gone rotten; with stains of moldy remains left behind, turned black from a once mildewed green, long ago. It's a rustic-quaint living space not meant for living but handy and dry! Where it's cold in Winter and cool in Summer! Where the décor includes quaint, once white now gray, heavily stained plastic lawn chairs with candles in bottles for light and ambiance! His abode considered *Sheik* in some circles and utilitarian with its cardboard boxes, newspapers, books, readily available. Now quickly notice the top of the apple-box that vintage, scratchy sounding AM/FM Transistor radio about glove size, playing Mozart! Do not snobbishly pass up his wardrobe made up of comfortable but worn, early Salvation Army Clothing with its distinguished tears, rips and smells of the Great Outdoors, *the gutter!* For ambiance slightly used coffee containers, and utilitarian plastic bags in case the need should arise. As if to add class to this marvel of a place frozen in time, a ratty clothesline with vintage wire hangers undulating in his drafty abode. Nate the traditionalist ignoring the use of lighter

9

weight but colorful plastic ones now in vogue.

Look above you! Stare through the moist-haze due to a total lack of heat. Heat what's that anyway to Nate? He forgot what that's like a long time ago except for Summers in quaint Washington Square Park and his Arch; which he feels he owns... He'd be glad to give you its History if you ask politely···And tell you that it was once made of wood, instead of *Stone!* Where nearby you'll notice his very own antiqued, flaky green park bench with handy *wastebasket*··· He hates that term, because he finds Treasures are to be found there··· half eaten sandwiches, perhaps part of an uneaten Hotdog, hopefully with a splash of mustard upon it. Frequently fries are found there due to the generosity of a passerby making a deposit in his food bin, probably watching their *Carbs... "The More the Merrier!"* He shouts when he finds them! *And* fries without flies are a veritable treasure of pleasure···Whoops! almost forgot dessert! Yes dessert! From the guilty Carb watcher a half-eaten, glazed donut, worth its weight in gold, or fancy Prune Danish that keeps your bowels regular and seems to have a soul, right in the middle where the prune delicacy lives··· It's a lucky day when he finds soda in a bottle or a container with coffee and a genuine plastic lid upon it making it even more desirable, adding a sense of purity to it... Nate chose this abode of his carefully for he needs to be surrounded by beauty. That background, that backdrop of trees, and grass some brown, some green, some patchy and un-seemly... Really!... This his current Dream, being surrounded by the wealth of West 4th of the once opulent Brownstones which he was impressed by, protected by, somewhat overwhelmed by. Yes out here in the hot hazy Summer where it gets boiling hot, in the Sun's embrace. But then that's when his abode the

Arch is most desirable. It is *Cool!*... Him with his delusions of grandeur, envisions his address to be #1- 5$^{\text{th Ave}}$ Once the address of a famous Nightery where Comedian Pat Carroll and other famous performers held forth... There in his salty days as an Educator-Orator-Philosopher-Sage, The Great Nate would hold forth over drinks, usually scotch, at the Bar with his friends, sometimes students··· Where in his glory days he felt as if he were the Oracle himself transmuted right out of the temple at Adelphi into the warm ambiance of # 1- 5th Ave. Oh yes he had an Big Ego then but *Life* can and usually does humble you! As it did Nate!... Who nowadays is loved, with friends galore in the Washington Square Park··· Great friends, more than just acquaintances, no time for just being casual. This business of staying alive here was real··· Here you could starve, or freeze, or rats make a meal of you. They like fingers and toes; I've been told or suffer heat stroke. Worse still die of addiction or Booze! Truly not the most prestigious ways to go! So these were pals and would give their last halfa stale donut and found-on a park bench chilled coffee, left behind by a sometimes charitable lady or guy who might just leave a half-eaten sandwich behind to keep it company··· Needless to say *Everyone* here likes Nate, they liked him back then··· when he was full of himself and seemed to know everything about everything··· Predicting things that sometimes came true. Hard to believe? But true! ···Oh yeah Nate shared with his pals, his buds, his friends. The animals, squirrels were nuts about him too, along with stray cats who looked to him for scraps. After all wasn't he a feral like them? This indigent, by choice, generous man. Dogs even showed their admiration by licking his bare feet at night. When they managed to sneak in through the sometimes open steel door. You see Nate had

11

no doorman, none to be found···

What is it about this NATE ?... Simply stated he is a Bearded, Pulitzer Prize Winner, former member of a D.C. Think Tank, his dubious age 55··· Generous, divorced, enigmatic, eccentric, elusive, reclusive; with repulsive body odor and holier than thou clothing. An escapee from the *Angst* of society. And The Distinguished 'Oracle of Was,' Nate Nicols, ex-professor, with a PhD in Sociology and knowledge of the Entire Universe under his stained baseball cap! Who has the propensity for and predilection for dereliction, now abiding in the Arch in Washington Square, NYC. Whiling away time, Reading-Sunning-Funning-Chatting-Advising, Living and *Derelicting!*... No need to mention here that *He* and his friends all had problems with Society; left it or abandoned by it!

There were marvelously interesting things about him especially his great knowledge and lore of the city. He knows his City··· This creature of God is like no other, Bodacious, Audacious and yet retiring··· in his own way, incredible. Who claims (it's since been verified) to have been a professor at Columbia, where not being able to stand the Northerly climes of New York's upper Westside later moved Downtown where he found it more comfortable to profess at NYU saying howdy do to the Bohemians there too···Nowadays any *so called Bohemians* have moved East to the East Village. Some went to Brooklyn, some upstate to Beacon and Woodstock··· Gotta keep moving they felt as the rents kept moving higher and higher···On the up-side; there is an upside!... For those that stayed, the street people found the quality of Food in dumpsters improved mightily but the competition for it *fierce!–*

-- Why you could starve in between if it wasn't for the Salvation Army and myriad charitable food pantries throughout the city who were feeling the pinch as more and more people were on the dole!... Nate, his friends and associates survive on them. God Bless'em or they'd all starve!···Not all like Nate, *chose* this fate, many of his friends being on rehab from drugs and alcohol! His friends are thankful to Nate--- he encourages them to stay clean···Ain't easy! Nothin's easy in this life nuthin!··· But Nate why he doesn't care nuthin about life no more···No way! Just takes it all in stride on the long ride through life.   Seen his share of strife···It's said he once had a wife, good woman too but even she couldn't understand his ways, his brilliance, his *ways!*··· He taught Sociology–Philosophy, minored in Life and knew quite a few well known types.   Coulda been a psychiatrist, brilliant, still brilliant···you don't   outgrow it--- *brilliance.* Never! not him anyway···He'll share it and himself with you for free or over a cupa coffee and sandwich, if you happen to have a roast beef one on you with a pickle in the middle's his favorite. You'll probably love him, most people do··· You'll begin to see he's trying to stay hidden in the Arch he claims for himself, his bastion against society! He's happiest there··· Funny thing about ole Nate··· He seems to know a lot about Historic; heinous things that happened close by his wonderful *Pad* and neighborhood; as fancy and as respectable as it once was··· If he were here would probably tell you this was a Hanging Ground for many poor souls on the wrong side of the Law who's fate was to be hung till dead and buried underfoot here or close by··· Sad but true! Then there was that terrible incident May 10th 1849 the time of the Bloody Theatrical *Riot* which turned into a *Massacre* on Astor Place not far from where the subway now stops. Over an argument about who was the greatest and more popular Actor, the Englishman William Macready or the famous American leading man Edwin Forrest, Tragedian and America's famous Shakespearean Actor at that time! As a result of that *Riot* 31 people were left dead. In fact one innocent lady sitting in a window blocks away was shot dead as she was gazing out.

A word to the curious if you ask him real nice like, maybe remember to bring along that roast beef sandwich and black coffee. He'll give you all the details and then some··· Why there's even this *Ghostly* story he tells about Alex··· Excuse me Alexander Hamilton who lived a short distance South-a-here who it seems got himself shot in a Duel over in Jersey with his archenemy Aaron Burr, never even got off a shot, himself they say!... Then his seconds and friends rowed him across the Hudson to his home near here and died shortly thereafter. Being gut shot in a Duel like the Great Russian Poet Pushkin is mighty painful from which it's said you die an agonizingly slow death··· Burr, fellow that shot him probably never grieved over that duel either. No love lost there!··· Sounds like I'm a teller of tales but you ask him he'll probably tell you that now not only does Alex wander these *Ghostly* green lawns in the park but is joined at times by John Barrymore famous Actor with a famous drinking problem himself, who had a pad nearby off the park rented from this sweet old gal··· One day decided to make a garden out of the roof using tons of dirt which nearly destroyed her house! Never again the Landlady could be heard saying. "*Never again!*"··· According to Nate, he came-a-calling to share the news with Nate and just be neighborly. Why he could write a book··· And once in awhile they tell him about things that are

14

going to happen in the future, there's a kind of Underground here where some say he heard about and was able to actually predict 911 a year ahead of time! Tried to get the authorities to listen··· And nobody did···Nate's famous for it but something no one would believe till after it was all over and too late to prevent. Imagine that? Now his meanderings are truthfully unveiled exposing his exciting life before your very eyes; but hold on to your heart you'll need to do that with Nate and Friends!

Chapter One

A Siren! Nate's Wakeup Call!

It's *Springtime*, but no time is a good time to wake Nate who grouchily jumps up, instantly awake wouldn't you be if 4 Fire trucks just whizzed by Sirens and Horns blasting you out of Rem Sleep? Something Nate our resident Oracle at Washington Arch never has gotten used to, try as he may. But a small price to pay for his rent free Flop, *pardon me Nate,* Abode! The hard concrete floor doesn't help much either along with his Vintage Flower Child bedroll with its Historically decorative stains, *(if it could only talk)* and which is presently Cohabitated by its tenants the centipedes and a few nonmalignant, he hopes, spiders. Our hero's life is simple lacking the complexities of every day cares and woes of the worker drones outside his Posh address, he proudly refers to as #1- 5th Ave!...

This is one Homeless Dude thankful to be alive and in reasonably good health--- free to do as he damn well pleases! Which includes his Daily Activities, like checking for the latest newspapers, coffee & bagels in the wastebasket near his, Abode in the Arch which he feels should be named Nate's Arch, seems that would be more appropriate, after all George Washington departed Mother Earth a long time ago! And Nate believes he's got Squatter's Rights with no Divs on his abode here! ... Nate is an enigmatic soul, a pretender to cleanliness; when you first see him in action *reminds you of Chaplin*...The way he moves, his gestures and mannerisms... Watch him carefully as he wets a paper towel with water from a glass jug; he's proud of that. The hell with plastic he's that kinda of *Guy.* Washes diligently around his eyes, portals to his immortal soul... So he can read the fine print in his latest supply of discarded New York Times and Village Voice Newspapers... Amongst his myriad other talents he vainly fancies himself a poet...No one else seems to, but he does that's the important thing. He's now ready to hang his damp paper towel on a ratty, yellow, plastic clothes line, to dry. "Waste not want not !" Where did he hear that? ... And too long ago to recollect. Time now to complete his TOILETTE de Bain in case he should meet anyone of importance while on his *very own* Park Bench where he holds *Court!...* Combs his hair now with a partial comb, with its remaining few teeth; straightens and diligently hand brushes his ratty clothes... Feeling cleansed and suitably dressed to hold Court is ready to face the World Outside he Loves!...The other

Mad World he could care less about which he abandoned a

longtime ago; though at times there are those nosey do-gooders who attempt unsuccessfully to bring him back to... Who know and at times he'll admit this himself, had so much to offer others. But felt others used him for their own selfish reasons who sought his Genius, knowledge, wisdom, for their own aggrandizement, edification, ...and cared nothing about him...M of whom felt had the gift of precognition, now more than in his early days...Truth be known *he* has no talent in that direction, merely friends in Low Places... For instance if you were to ask him about the company he keeps, would freely admit to knowing Alexander Hamilton and John Barrymore who would frequently share Historic and Theatrical vignettes with him and at certain times because they were in a *Psychic Pipeline* would predict the future...*Like*, and you're not gonna believe this... 911! ... Yes 911 a year to the date which he attempted to warn the cities fathers about along with the Pentagon, the President, the CIA, NSA, and FBI!... Did we miss anything ?... Naturally all took him for a Madman! Wouldn't you? ...Why he even gave them details that he was given by John and Alex....No one to a man or woman believed him would you? A man who appeared to have lost his senses living as a semi-recluse in the Arch, a derelict though, once acknowledged genius in his field, an esteemed, at one time Professor Emeritus in: Sociology, Phycology, and Logic! He was and is quite a man, an *Oracle*... it's believed by many.

To a loud Cacophonic-Fanfare of Birds, Squirrels, dogs barking, horns and Sirens Blowing as if to trumpet his entrance to 'Life in the Park,' as the Oracle of Was enters his Throne Room the *Park* in all its glory and begins his day. Nate making his grand entrance into the World at large. A man appearing mad but a Genius nevertheless who's clock is on Daylight Saving when the Rest of the world's on Standard Time! He sings as he leaves the Arch and enters his Living/Throne Room--- 'The Park' where life throbs for him, happily accepting his Enigmatic Station ... Stepping out happily, stiffly, coldly, seeking warmth, into the mild spring air with the Sun breaking through, in the smoggy East. His Court showing him homage, respect, as Squirrels stop gathering nuts long enough to bark a welcome, birds singing beautifully more profoundly now, while pigeons join in the symphony to announce their friends arrival with the new comers the Sea gulls who see him as a friend and benefactor who shares with all the world, bar none... Why even Rats find room in their heart for this man that shares his last crust with them. Treat him kindly and do not nibble on his toes or fingers while he sleeps, as if to show the respect they feel for him. Grandly now he approaches His Throne, The Bench! His subjects waiting and visiting as the day progresses, weather permitting... Then after a moment to recap his daily agenda. Walks stiffly, if not stately over to the wastebasket looks in, finds a half spent container of coffee and a partially eaten bagel... In ecstasy now! Sets his prized breakfast down beside him on the Throne. Once again rising slowly, old bones, muscles not responding too rapidly; creakily stretches as fully as nature allows; hobbles over, does he remind you of Chaplin by any chance? Like Chaplin he has a lot of the Clown in him... Perhaps he imagines he has an audience? Actually he does!... His friends! Almost as if he's the Modern day St. Francis, but no Saint he, not this man. At times if his homeless friends in the park sleepily arising see their Buddy through mucous encrusted eyes, manage a wave? No dialogue necessary here all know each other and their plight...Respect in their humble way other's plights... Many of whom tend to be highly territorial about the park. Well he is too, but always shares when able. Happy to be alive, greets the morn; mockingly attempts the stretches as he's seen joggers do...Decides now that he's fully awake to brush the bench off scrupulously, spots a speck on the bench; brushes it with his cuff. Then realizes his first duty should be to thank his Maker! And welcome the Sun's warmth and light; the better to read by; his preoccupation that, and to protest, when a good cause presents itself!   This to him is living and profound!

This typical day begins with a bold-bright, if not slightly hazy Sun shining. He starts things off after dining on his meager breakfast. Now fully prepared to greet his friends who slowly almost dreamlike, still half asleep, but always willing to help their leader Nate with this gathering of their revered Sunshine Club to welcome old Sole with their almost daily ritual, as they might in the Florida Keys... sans booze. To kick off their day with just being free spirits and souls before their Maker, who they all basically believed in, perhaps were instructed in, if they didn't always practice his precepts.

All his aches and pains discarded now as Nate *passionately,* leaps onto his bench, singing out! "I salute you Sun, as I fly into the *Breach* of a glorious new day!" As he looks to the East, salutes, doffs hat then bows addressing the Sun grandly! "Thank You! for your sweet, warm light this morning... After a night in my icy Abode in the Arch!" Now Dutifully *massages* his bod... *"Oooh!* That feels sooo... goood!... Is that Thunder rumbling?... *God!* I'm not forgetting You! Good Morning and thanks! I'm not an ungrateful bum, just a poor one; by choice! By choice!" Arms now stretched skyward... To 'The WAS,' the Arch he affectionately calls by that appellation, "good morning my love! Blows her a kiss... You Pigeons, I've not forgotten you; show respect, hold your fire! Pigeon doo draws my Ire!... We're all friends heeere"--- drags it out for effect. Pigeons like that! "And that includes my Squirrely pals, whom I implore; do not your nuts, upon my head keep score!... To the

World at large, I say! No need to fear! Nate's still here!... Oracle and Guardian of the People! Defender of Park benches and people's rights. Welcoming *All* to Washington Arch Square in the Village, my Abode! Which I Happily share with my indigent companions: poets, actors, musicians, artists, dreamers and --- lovers! And lest I forget passersby!" ... Carried away, he *Sings!* Loudly!... " New York ! New York! What a Marvelous Town! Simply Marvelous Town!" ... Almost angrily, loudly shouts with a mixture of love and affection, he's a little mad, just a little... "LISTEN! Listen out there to those Sirens, my Lorelei sings to me--- beckons to me! Luring me onto the Rocks of Depravity--- Manhattan's sidewalks, streets and gutters!... Damn! Damn! Damn! Keeping me up at night, getting me up in the morning! Serenading at all hours, every day, of the bloody year. But Thank God for that or our buildings would all burn down!" ... Now with great concern speaks of the plight of His Proud City the Country ... " With Her Firemen, Her Cops; 24-7 on the job keeping us safe, always prepping and protecting against the possibility of a *New Terrorist Attack!*" ... You see no War's too little to make Nate's Blood Pressure and Temper flare! Which now seems to be The War on Terror!

"*Hey! Nate!* You shoulda run for office!" This from his *Bud* and confidant Harry happily sauntering by, with a busy day planned. And just happened to catch the end of Nate's Solo act, with only a few of his irregulars present... None of his friends having showed up for the *Greet the Sun Ritual* of their Sunshine Club. Harry lovingly carrying a huge black plastic bag of money; that is to say deposit cans and bottles. You know he's gotta comment and rib Nate sooo, "You act like you're The Mayor of Washington Square!... Do I care? Hell no!... Now I'm the Poet and you sound like a politician Nate!... Sorry I missed your Ode to the Sun, thing... but, me, I've got work to do, people to see, deposit cans to cash in on, and an Egg Mac Muffin and coffee to actually buy and feast on! Oh yes, I got a Big Day planned!"

"Bout time!" Nate counters "Duty first!... Sir Harry don't sully my reputation by laying insults on me! How gross! *Me* as a Politician? Perish the thought! As he steps gingerly down, as he sips his coffee, and acquired trait... Want a slug of coffee?

"Nah! I've had an appetizer, found some, still warm coffee on a park bench. Somebody left in a hurry. Sorry! thought I was throwin you a compliment Nate, my man! As they High 5 each other.. You're loved by all of us inhabitants, junkies, drunks, *Can* & bottle collectors like me, even squirrels! Why you'd win hands down! I'd be first in line to vote for you... because of your darlin' smile, and winning ways!

"Thanks!... *Now, who* sounds like a politician?"

"Not me!" Harry affirms!... "Harry before you toddle off... Where in Hell are the regulars of Our Sunrise Club?"

Shrugging, "*Dunno!*... But see you later, gotta go on my appointed rounds. Deposit Cans & Bottles are impatient for ownership and if I don't collect them first, they show no loyalty

and some other Bum will have his way with them and get the deposit...Adios!"

Shouts after him, "Good luck with your Loot!" Announcing loudly to anyone who cared to listen. "Could be Mary slept in or was *Arrested* for vagrancy in another surreptitious Sweep of *The WAS!*... *'Washington Arch Square!'* Which I loudly *proclaim, even if I'm called MAD!*... Once the Bohemian Mecca of NYC!... You

22

gotta know that most Poor *Skids* with any sense at all took off for the East Village years ago... Except for wealthier sidewalk aristocrats like me, with a 5th Ave. address and such good friends as Harry and Mary, living off the land-and-hand of Charity. I'll bow to that!" Being the Ham he is! "But who can afford it?"... Looking up to the Sun, implores it, " less light, please!" The Sun seems to obey almost immediately and goes behind a cloud. Nate's got powers he's not even tapped yet... "Thanks!" *Ceremoniously sits,* reaches for breakfast, crosses legs, reads newspaper, mumbles, disturbed by the news, loudly decares! "Are they *Nuts?*"... Notices his friend the squirrel. Not you my friend!"... Which causes the Squirrel to mumble something under his breathe, not printable... " *First* they build a Sports Arena in Brooklyn and displace, dispossess, complaining residents that had no clout; to fight the elite with the ones with all the money and power. *Greed!* that's what it's all about!... Before you know it they'll build a bridge over the Hudson; call it The George Washington!" As he *Convulses over his (he thinks) joke.* " Ha! ha! ha!" ... Then stiffly *Stands.* "Maybe I should do standup?--- but... **Sitting Down!** Sits suddenly... *changes* his mind, leaps up on the bench, agitated. Then Speaks of *George,* the one from Texas!... **"W"**... Why'd we ever go to War?... What's that? *Weapons* of mass *what?* ... Sea Gulls annoyed with his diatribe, try to quiet their friend down with their Caw! Caw! *Caws!* As if to remind Nate that's old News, Pal!... Get a Life!... Suddenly! *Wildly throws arms, with clenched fists up to the sky and shouts!* "It's a toss of the Dice where our troops will land, or Drones attack!" Imagines he hears a Drone overhead and Marching feet of a huge Army. " **Harch! 2-3-4! Harch, 2-3........!"** *Passersby wondering is this Man is Losing It?*

 The Jogger

THIS HAPPENS TO BE a special, eventful morning for our Oracle though not aware of anything special as along comes someone very special to most folks in the City innocently jogging along. Is it? Why yes it is the Mayor of NYC himself! Don't tell anyone but this is no coincidence. Though he does live in the West Village and tries to keep his aging body in some kind of shape by jogging the Cities' streets unmindful of security or bodyguards or any other serious threats to his wellbeing or office… A politician always anxious to get a handle on the people he watches over. More like a loving, caring, almost nonpolitical Politician, if that's possible. The Mayor now pushing 55, a happy go lucky, loved by his constituency Man of the people by the people and for the people… Who though friendly, outgoing, and pleasant is a firm leader, and now surreptitiously seeking out the Oracle of Was. Having heard unbelievable tales of the Enigmatic Man rumored to be an Oracle from some Greek Temple at Adelphi, pure hype they say but he might just be legitimate. His mission today… to befriend Nate and drain his brain for the good of the City and Country … Having been inspired by his abilities… this 'Oracle of WAS,' famed for his 911 prediction which at the time was not believed until after the horrific event. .. And now that he believes he's found his Oracle, moves in on him like a bird of prey while Nate is sunning his aching body in the park! And carefully approaches him attracted by Nate's mumblings and marching. He turns on his natural charm spoken in strict New Yorkeese with a slight aura and flavor of Jewish hutzpah. "Good Morning! And please save the 'Gee, don't I know you from somewhere?... Everyone in New York City knows me. Why shouldn't they? I'm Mayor Ed Koach!... Besides no one else looks this old and wrinkled at 55! ... Mind if I sit a minute?"

Nate, Mr. noncommittal... only- gestures it's OK!

"I knew right away you looked familiar!... 'The Oracle of WAS!'... sometimes found on the front page of The Village Voice or The Times! I'll try not to interfere with your reading, ranting, marching, arithmetic and breakfast... Or sound like a politician. What was that Rhetoric about anyway?"

Slightly facetious; begrudgingly answers? "The *state* the World's in! You name it!... I'm damned angry!... Mr. Mayor I gotta say you must be hard up, stopping *here,* to get my vote!... By the way, if you're the Mayor; I'm Vice President, Nate Nicols, at your service. How do you do? Strange we haven't met in NYC, or during one of your visits to D.C. but I know you by your pictures." *He's usually this way with politicos...* "on the *back* page of the Times!"

"Look! As any good Politician whom you evidently despise knows, I have my spies. And found out about your great reputation as a sage educated philosopher, Oracle, ex-professor, Pulitzer Prize winning acclaimed personage and predictor of 911 whom nobody acceded or paid attention to, much to the embarrassment of just about anyone in authority in the US and

NYC, did I leave anything out?"

"Just one or two things, one *I'm Retired,* and two really don't give two toots for the political scene and the weirdo's that run this Country! But having slowed down, don't do many protest marches. Too old! Less of course it's close to my heart."

They shake hands. "A pleasure meeting the park's *distinguished* ex-professor, Think Tank Persona, and Pulitzer Prize winning, PhD habitué."

"Some would like to see me as the *extinguished,* habitué. And remember never to wash that hand, when you get back to City Hall!"

"Never!" *As he playfully stares at it.*

"Good! You know, even with the shades

you do bear a resemblance to Mayor *Roach!"*

"Mayor Ed Koach--- Koach! With a K!" *While he makes himself identifiable by taking off his sunglasses.*

Naturally Nate, feigns surprise. " It is you!... I suggest you put'em back on! It gives you more of a debonair flair!... I'm convinced now, though I had my doubts... It's a pleasure meeting you Mayor, though; I don't always agree with you!"

" What's not to agree with? I'm dogmatic, good looking with my hairpiece on, look and act smart in my Armani suits. Have my BS, MS, PhD, LLB; and MTA! And believe in a government by the people"... *Always milks humor from the spoken word.* "And for *some* of the people."

"Very creative!... I have some of those... a BS, MS, PhD, and slept on the finest MTA trains. I was just expressing my reaction to Politicos as a HOLE! A Void!... While reading the News Politicians who have nothing better to do than spend taxpayer money, on ill-advised Wars in the Middle East.   When we could've used sanctions and containment. Like We did with Russia during the cold war!... And Damn it! Spend that money to rebuild our Infrastructure!"

" A great idea Nate; but you're talking to the Mayor, you need a Congressman."

"That's called passing the buck!...Whatever happened to the Buck Stops here!"

"The Buck does stop here in New York City --- My Beat! *Not* the Nation! I believe you missed your calling you *should'a* been a politician! … But *Back* to the present; are you aware I jog here mornings and live nearby?"

"I've heard."

"Do you begin to suspect this meeting is not by chance?"

"Not really, why meet with a bum like me?"

"I've heard stories about a sage street-person, an *Oracle*, living in the Arch in Washington Square. A genius, renowned Professor and a Think Tank PhD, sometimes consulted by World Leaders. Who would have made a wonderful CEO or at least a wonderful Politician! And is clairvoyant, so the *Myth* goes."

"The Myth is part true, part legend. Yes, I was a Sociology Prof., *never* a politician or CEO. Let me say if I were a CEO, I 'd feel guilty having a ridiculously high salary, stock options and a Golden Parachute; plucked from workers, and stockholders pockets… Not to boast, but if *I* were Mayor, this city would flourish and be profitable... However, I'm *not* clairvoyant. Your sources were as misinformed as the Ex-President!"

" Ha! And for your information the city makes no profit!"

" It should! It would save *taxpayers* a bundle."

" Ha! That... From one who never files!"

"Degrading, but true!... *Honestly,* I used to file... *honestly!*"

"Good for you!... Why am I doing this?... Having this weighty conversation with a park bench ideologue?"

" You chose to!... Remember?... Realizing that through some fluke, you've finally met up with someone who *knows* what the Hell he's talking about!"

"All day long I speak with people who claim to *know* what the *Hell* they're talking about; mostly politicians. Why do you think you're different?"

" Because I'm not a politician! Therefore have the advantage of higher education, experience, common sense... even wisdom! Have no agendas, and cater to no lobbyists... *Escaped* all that, years ago."

"If my Staff could hear this discussion; they'd send me off for Psychiatric Evaluation... *Back* to the reason I'm here... Did you actually predict 911 a year before it happened?"

" As to your Staff, after they got to know this over educated, enigmatic, escapee from Society they'd realize that I've much to impart to that gang of misfits... Probably would insist on me running for the Presidency, to fix the Country!... And *Yes!* I predicted 911.... Notified the FBI, New York's Finest and the CIA, and NSA; but they'd have none of it. Even wanted to Institutionalize me!... Forgetting they don't have 'Nuthouses anymore.' Except in 'The WAS,' with my friends the Squirrels; or is it Squirrelly friends?... So... I stopped informing and am Happy in The WAS!"

" This from a park bench Oracle, tell me! Would *you* have believed *you*?"

"Certainly!"

"How'd you come up with the prediction?"

"Hard to explain to a nonbeliever. It was *not* of this World! But from Alex, who heard it through *the Underworld's Grapevine!*"

"The Underworld?"

"Alex's friends are from there!"

"The Underworld?... Are you talking about a subversive organization? Like a threat to National Security? If it is we'll *bust* it wide open! Give me the facts! I'll see to it these terrorists are arrested!"

"You'll need a pickax and shovel!"

"Stop clowning! Where exactly is this Underworld located?"

"*Underground!*...You're standing on it! Make no *bones* about it! Pardon the pun, but this was a burial ground. *He indicates approximately where.* "They hung condemned prisoners at a nearby gallows, and buried them in a Potters field here... In fact there's a huge Underworld population here of restless spirits, angry as Hell! Because they got hung in their

29

prime."

The Mayor is by now *Simmering!* "*Tilt!* ... Sorry, I thought I was talking to a rational man."

"Wouldn't go that far; but some things I know. One of which is, Alex is *never* wrong! It's his gift to be able to foretell the future. I merely passed along the info and everyone figured me demented!... Though like most geniuses I'm seen as eccentric and an enigma... Long story short; no one listened though I tried."

"Alex, is a tough pill to swallow, and *you're* not easy... I believe that there's truth, to the *Myth*. And you do have a gift, or Alex does... Therefore have a proposition: Would you mind if I told my compatriots about you? After putting me in a straitjacket, I have a feeling they'd want me to bounce some issues off you and... er...Alex."

"It's Crazy!... I'd don't mind... Just keep the damn Media away!... Don't need'em badgering me! I'm too busy... have no time for Idiots!"

"It's a deal. In fact just the other day the Governor said to me; Mayor Roach, err...Koach; sometimes I wish I had someone like Solomon to go to for advice, or like the ancient Greeks, an Oracle... Now I go back to him and what do I say?"

"Solomon I'm not!" *Says it slowly savoring it.*"Oracle's Good!   Actually people around here and elsewhere, I understand have been calling me that for quite a while. Kinda like it too, it smacks of *Psychic* knowledge, the Paranormal and mysterious power. Apropos too, because, I'm always talking to *Wise* spirits of the dead, in my 'Temple of Apollo'--- THE WAS."

"Then ORACLE and 'THE WAS'... it is!... Fascinating!... Till next time! Err... how do I contact you?"

"Ask anyone in the park, even cops... On a good day you'll find me right here sunning, reading... If I'm lucky, eating."

"Alright then! I'll soon bring you back the Governor's *bag* of trick questions."

" Excellent! ... Speaking of Bags would it be too much trouble to bring me a *bag* lunch with a roast beef sandwich on rye, a Dill and coffee, black?"

" You bet!"

" Better mention the tough questions may take awhile... Cause I need time to confer with Alex."

"Naturally!"

"Make that Supernaturally Mayor!"

"Take care of yourself. You're precious to us! See you soon!" *Ed Koach our man of the People and for the Straphangers, as New York Subway Riders are sometimes amicably called, unceremoniously jogs off through the Park.*

Chapter Two

NAN!

A little later in his very busy day carousing, reading, communing with people, birds and squirrels: *Nan saunters on from just across West 4th St.* and only a few yards away from Nate's abode making the journey from her very own Brownstone left to her by her deceased husband. A wealthy guy with lots of money and many choice real estate holdings. Nan happens to love Nate in fact is mad about him. However Nate being too busy being independent at the moment at least treats her merely as a good friend, he refuses anything else.

" Mornin' Nate!... Who was that?"

"The Mayor!"

" Sure! And I'm Secretary of State."

"Nah! You've "got a much better figure."

"Thanks! If that's a compliment."

He's nothing if not fast... "It is! You have! And you're welcome!"

"Seriously who was that? He looked familiar, is it the guy that has the greasy spoon on West Eighth?"

Shakes his head violently, *No!* "I doubt he has any greasy spoons. It was the Mayor. Couldn't you tell by his nostrils?"

"His nostrils?"

"Yes!... He has two."

"How weird! I knew there was something peculiar about him!"

"Actually not bad for a politician."

"What did he want?"

He Curtsies holding an imaginary skirt. "Guess he liked my smile, demeanor and stylish clothing! After we talked ... was apparently impressed by my genius, my affability, honesty and anxiously seeks my advice, and counsel! Not just for himself mind, but his political cronies... Wanted to know if I'd mind giving my Oracle like wisdom a tweak, and answer some problematic questions... I said sure, but it'll cost you a roast beef sandwich, coffee black, and a Dill to match my personality, sour!. A small price to pay for sagacious, genius like answers, from Old Nate."

Shakes her head with disbelief, sighs... " I Can't believe my good friend, whom I wish were more than, that is after a good cleaning up, and remaking of your exterior, would sell your genius so cheaply to the first bidder. Why you don't even know the man, and you're selling your mind for a roast beef sandwich?... Nate you're my best pal, going way back to College, as my Professor, my Mentor.

"As Henry the Fifth once said 'My Horse! My Horse! My kingdom for a Roast Beef Sandwich! Or was that the Inventor of the Sandwich... The Earl of Sandwich? ... Hmmm?...."

"For once can't you be serious? As I was lamenting my confessor, soothsayer and Psychic and... Wow, we really do go back far. Time must be flying and leaving us in the dust!"

"You don't have to be flip about it! As for me I'm feeling good about us rekindling our friendship since our meeting last year here in Beautiful 'Was.' "

"And you living right across West 4th Street... Neighbors and didn't even know it."

" Yeah! Me in my little Brownstone still carrying a torch for Nate in your little Arch... My Mentor and friend living like a derelict with all your genius... And obviously not feeling about me the way I feel about you... I'm announcing here and now I'm not giving up on you my sweet. And am appointing myself guardian of your life, liberty, *welfare, happiness* and *soul* which I hate to see you *Shill* for a *Dill!*"

"Aah! But there's a sandwich and coffee in it too as my reward. And if you have any inkling of what makes up politicians daily lives you *know* they're constantly being bombarded by problems. And this is His Honor the Mayor we're talkin' about here, who seems to care about his Strap-Hangers. so naturally I said bring'em on!"

"If you have such low esteem, perhaps your price might be too high after all?"

"Yeah! The coffee'll probably put him in arrears."

She *Dramatically* lifts skyward a bag with goodies in it. "Speaking of which, I brought my favorite Oracle a prized bag with a toasted Sesame bagel in it, which you have a love hate relationship with because of its many carbs.. I know you object vehemently when I bring you *food*... Want it?"

"It's a guy thing! Sure!" But gladly Takes it. " It'll go fine with my haul this morning, I found a treasure; a half a donut and half a hot dog... So Thanks!"

Nods her head solemnly. "Mmm! Life is good!...And I knew, though you never saw me; Nan the student, as being infatuated with you, that someday you'd grow to appreciate me."

Nods, sagely... "That's obviously the Psychic you with your feminine intuition on overload! Yes, I appreciate you, but then, you always were a likeable, very bright student of mine, and never saw you as anything else; though a few times I caught you staring at my brow!"

Shakes her head yes then walks quietly over to him and takes his motely, dirty but nevertheless friendly hand! "Hm, Hmm! First I fell in love with your brain then your brow. Before I realized how lovable your whole being was, and still is!"

"You're my best pal Nan; you know that, even if you do wear clean panty hose every day; have clean underwear and stockpiles of wealth and townhouses...The toughest thing for me to fathom is why you need to bathe every day?"

"I happily plead guilty! So I have a few trivial real estate holdings. Can I help it, if I inherited an expensive Greek Revival Brownstone across the street. *No!* And a small 24 room shack in South Hampton, that happens to be on the Ocean... And is it my fault my deceased husband liked real estate? So, I have lots and lots of lots! And what's wrong with bathing daily and wearing clean pantyhose every day? And underwear? You should try it!"

"Pantyhose, *never!*... Bathing *hardly* ever! Clean underwear would make me itch... It's the detergent you know!"

Steps toward him takes both of his hands and warmly says, "but let's get back to my favorite question."

"Not that one!"

She kisses him on his bearded cheek, which he magnanimously allows. " Hmm, hmmm. Yes that one! For the umpteenth time prove you're my dear friend by getting off the street, and come home with me and live in a civilized fashion. Where I will warmly *Welcome* you! *Love* you! as a house guest as long as *death and taxes do not us part!*"

"I don't wanna be civilized!... Look! You have a loving heart, but I love *freedom,* no strings...no attachments, *no taxes!*"

"Begins to lose it. "*No! No! No!* That's not freedom! That's not civilized! That's irresponsible!... Get serious about yourself; and start living like a human! This is so beneath you!... Why can't you envision it Nate? ... You and Me together? ... We get along real well; you gotta admit that!... And *No* strings!"

"No thanks! Yes! I'm irresponsible. That's OK! It's my choice, no one else's.... If I can't kid life; life's gonna kid me, and *kick* me right in the ass!... As for your other expectations... Not for me!... Not interested!... Left all that!... Love it out here with my friends, my liberty, and pursuit of irresponsibility!"

"Street people, pigeons, seagulls and squirrels; you call friends? That's liberty?

"Free to be me! To greet my Maker and the Universe every morning... Yes friends! The birds the animals and my good Friends the Street people! And don't forget, Alex & John *my* very own *spooks.* The Sunrises, The Sunsets!... Liberty means many things, like newspapers to read. *My* park bench, a stale bagel and coffee in the morning. The World is my *acorn*---Yours claustrophobic, paranoiac, angst ridden. People rushing about, worrying *where* their next cupa coffee is coming from, and if they need a loan to pay for it?... I say give me Liberty with *No DEBT!*

"*Damn!* You call that liberty, are you *nuts?* Your balls are in a vice here!"

"Ouch!... Careful you're getting testicular!... Nan! I don't wanna live in your Brownstone! Don't wanna be "civilized." Even if it *does* mean only moving across the street from here, from Washington Square...Besides you'd come home, find my friends sleeping on the floor; eating you outa house and refrigerator. *Including* your caviar and imported Foie Gras. Might even have squirrels cracking their nuts on the living room rug. We can't have that! ... Now can we?"

"You're right about that! It's *you* I want, not your street people, or squirrelly friends cracking their nuts on the living room rug!

"Nah!... Wouldn't work! I left all that craziness, couldn't

stand it, too confining! ... Let's just stay friends."

She finally but only temporarily Acquiesces. "Oh, Nate!"

"That's the way it's gotta be!

"Look! I'm tired of trying... Doesn't mean I'm giving up though!... See *you* later!" Sounds more like a threat!... *Then stalks off in a huff, back to her Brownstone.*

"Later it is!"...Coolly sits down on his marvelous Throne, a finer Park Bench you'll not find anywhere! One that would make Henry the Fifth proud and the Earl of Sandwich! Relaxes, reads, and sips coffee. Glad the discussion is over for the umpteenth time. Aah he thinks... she's a good friend though!"

Harry-Himself !

Harry *energetically*, you could say proudly meanders over from the other end of the park where his abode, a newly painted, pickle green Park Bench stands boldly against the elements... which coincidentally happens to match a 3 day old pickle he just discovered. And sings out for all the world to hear,   if   they   wish!
"Hey Nate! What a haul of Deposit cans and bottles I had. Made myself some Big money... How ya doin'?"

"Great! But too bad you couldn't've been around for the Sunrise service!"

"Sorry about that but it was the maids day off!... Had to make my own bed and comb my unruly hair, got a late start! And Now Ladies and gentlemen thanks to the generosity and frivolity of humans have acquired enough wealth to buy breakfast.

"Yeah it's hard to get good help nowadays."

"Oh Nuts!! Just remembered! It's gonna ruin a perfect day for me too!... My Ma, I love her but she's relentless and comes lookin' for me about this time every month... When she gets her Social Security check, it reminds her to try and get me to come home. And I ain't goin Nate! I ain't goin!"

"Why not Harry? 3 squares a day, and then get yourself a good teaching job."

"As a grunt second lieutenant in Iraq and Afghanistan, had enough with the special meals, compliments of Uncle Samuel before you and your buddies got blown up by an IED!... And of course there were the delightful Chef's Choice Field Rations ... A pure delight! And you gotta be kidding as far as goin back to teaching, and *Marriage?*... Why I call that *civilized Jail!*" So as De Niro would say, " Figet about it!"

"You're beginning to sound like me Harry. Give me liberty and a park bench!"

HIs angst building now in anticipation. "Hey! Sssh, sssh! She could be seeking me out as we speak!   Gotta sneak off now, keep a low profile, try to avoid her!"

Plays along, "Sssh!...Gotcha!"

Harry quickly surveying the *park.* Woo-aah! I see someone across the park could be Ma! Uh, oh!... Nice talkin' to you Nate. Pardon my dust, doubt she saw me, she's near sighted. If she should ask my whereabouts... Say you don't know! He quickly takes off in the other direction as surreptitiously as possible.

"Good luck! See ya later!" Crosses his legs assumes his most relaxed mood and coolly *resumes reading.*

Three Siren toots later! Along comes Mary, a bright girl on rehab and a solid, faithful member of The Washington Arch Sunshine Club wandering on from Sullivan St. "Mornin Nate!... Sleep well your Lordship?"

Stretches, yawns before he gets up energy to answer her. "I get kinda lazy relaxing in the Sun." Manages to mumble. "And yes thanks but you can dispose of the formalities! Slept not too badly considering those damn sirens raising Hell all night? It's gettin' so's a body has to move to Poughkeepsie to find peace."

"Nah now they even got Sirens in Poughkeepsie, so I been told. I'll go with ya to the moon Nate! Even Poughkeepsie! If we gotta? But if you go take me wit ya!"

"Gotta be my Musk! Smells his armpits to make a statement ! Makes all you ladies want my love and of course my withered, emaciated, scarred body! What's wrong with just being friends? I'm good with that! By the way what would we live on... green cheese? You know I don't wanna be tied down, though you're a sweetheart... Hell! Where would I get the Times and the Wall Street Journal? By the time I got the news

40

the West Village would be underwater, from, Global warming!"

"They got them papers up there too!"

"Yeah but ya gotta buy' em.

"Here, they're free at a waste basket near you--- if you get lucky."

" Just so's you know if you decide to leave, I go with ya!... I want ya ta know it ticks me off, how cozy you are with that rich Bitch, Nan...I'm surprised ya haven't taken up house keepin' with that *Witch* with her money and real estate... *You Mister!* are my Guru, my Oracle, friend, financial adviser, my everything, ever since you came to 'The WAS,' I fell for you right off the bat!... I love you, my friend and you can't do nuthin about it except to except me! So there!... *Yes!* I 'm jealous, of that rich Witch wit a capital B an' I ain't apologizin!"

"No need, You're a good friend, and you're wrong about her and me. It's platonic...Let's *you* and me keep it that way too, Ok?

"Not OK! But I don't have no choice...Whatcha eatin'?"

"Here have half a my half-a-hotdog and some delicious, cold coffee to wash it down!"

"Oh alright!" Takes the offering, feeling some guilt about taking his meager offerings...But their rules are simple in the Sunshine Club they are all friends and simply, humbly share, even if they have to get by on a meager supply of eats themselves...

Mary on a roll rattles on, "why that rich *Bitch* didn't bring ya none of this, did she? If she did, I don't want any!"

"Nah just the coffee... *Not* to worry! It isn't poisoned even if she did handle it. She's my one and only rich Bitch but good friend. But you Mary, are rich in a different way. You have a rich soul and a heart."

"How can you stand to be within sniffing distance of that broad with her classy perfume, even her underarm deodorant is from Sach's 5th... She starts to settle down a little sits, crosses her legs like any good swell should and drinks her--- what she considers to be contaminated coffee, beggars as they say can't be choosey and snacks. "Go on I'll bet you tell that to all your ex-junkie females!"

"Only the ones named Mary! So you're the first, Darlin! No one else. We're kindred souls, you and me, for different reasons. But like you, need my freedom--- *no* ties! We could never bond beyond, being friends... I think you sense that?"

Rises suddenly crosses to him raises her voice louder than usual, "Sense...Schmentz!...I'm past that. I like ya too much. I wanna be close to you." Sidles up to him, he resists............

"Can't you see? Mary I like you as a friend, that's all I'm capable of. This is a great compliment you pay me but I'm not worth your affection."

"Don't tell me you ain't worth my affection! Let me be the judge of how worthless you are! Mr. Oracle! Because your most outstanding virtue is that you are the kindest man I know. You'd share your last crust wit the likes-a-me; your last sip of stale, Bitch contaminated coffee wit me... Ya know... what's the matter with you?"

"I give up?"

"Nothing a good shrink couldn't fix... I'm dead serious. And your honesty is to honest!... Damn it!"

"Please Mar no more talk of love! We're Buds. Let's keep it

that way!... So, Mar what are you up to?"

"Never mind what I'm up to! A girl can hope can't she?... Mister change-the-subject... And I can be as silly as you... 'Five foot two with eyes- a- blue'...Like that old song goes... What am I up to? You're always changin' the subject when I bring up a relationship... Ok I can play that game to!... this is my three 'S' day; I'm gonna go to the Shelter, get a Shower, and Schmooze; for dessert, get some counseling. After which Mr. Guru. I'll while away my time at the *library* improving my mind"

"Sounds like an *exciting* day!"

Says it like a SWELL, she thinks... and *mimics* Nate's other pal Nan. "If you'd like to meet me at the library later *Dahling,* you may. Say about noon. If you're not *too* busy Sweetheart?" Wipes mouth on sleeve, gets up, saunters seductively off like a classy, society type.

As she's leaving explains, "Sorry Mar, I have to catch up on my reading. I've accumulated a huge stockpile of newspapers." *Loudly adds!* "And *gotta* check the market in my Wall Street Journal."

A short time later Harry breathing hard comes jogging back to Nate, reporting in; "I'm back Professor! Finally eluded my Ma."

"Harry my friend it sounds like you outran that Lovely mother of yours. And don't call me Professor! My neighbors might think I'm an intellectual. Or...for spite ... I might retaliate and call out to you! HEY TEACH! … *That said*… I Got some food here you're welcome to share… By the way, Mary just split."

Sits down on Nate's bench. "It's a deal then I won't call you Professor if you don't call me Teach? Though I was a damned good English teacher… And I know the grapevine has it that you were this great Professor!"…

Nate silently acknowledges with a slight nod of his scruffy head… "But Harry we both lucked out here… someone left a donut on my bench." Unwraps it carefully, gives half to Nate.

"Why Thank you Sir! It looks like Steak to me!... Wow! What a great collection of papers you have here. Life is good! You must have the best source of the finest papers in the Square, right here!... Mind if I share?"

" Go right ahead. But I do, don't I. Why only the elite dump in my waste basket. Help yourself." They relax, eat and read together like the Pals they are.

"Nate you didn't even ask me how my Drug Rehab went this morning."

"Harry I've been meaning to do just that. So how did it go?"

"Well, the Methadone Rehab for this ex-teacher, ex-grunt with P.T.S. Syndrome, method actor; famous from one end of off-off Broadway to the Hudson River went swimmingly!"

" That's great! As your reward I'll treat you to brunch my friend. Veteran with a Bronze Star, P.T.S. and Method Actor on Methadone."

" Thanks!... I earned it! Wow! Am I excited!... I'm making great progress."

"Then you'll be leaving us, going back to teaching, making an honest living, back to the old *Rat race,* the *Human race;* living at home with your Ma? Will be sorry to see you go, but extremely happy for you!"

"Hell no, *Nate!*...Bite your tongue!…I love this life! It has its down side, but I love it!...With its lack of Stress, money! Angst, money! Pressure, money! And wouldn't trade it for all the diamonds in Africa. Or teaching jobs."

Pleased, rises goes to him shakes his hand and warmly congratulates Harry! "You're a man after my own heart... neither would I!... I selfishly must add I'm glad you're staying, you're one of my finest acquaintances."

"Glad you said acquaintances; it has a distant, cool ring to it, no long term friendships should be made in 'The WAS!' Keep your plastic garbage bag packed, and ready to move on at any time, kinda *feel* to it.

"That's why we get along so well Har... On that note, I hate to eat and break this off but it's getting late. Have to spiff up my abode, read and rest, listen to classical music on my faithful, scratchy transistor radio... Adios Amigo!"

"See ya tomorrow, enjoy your musical interlude... Ok if I borrow your bench?"

"With my blessings, while you're at it; use some of my reading materials to keep off the foggy, foggy dew!" Harry Rises, Nate hands him newspapers as Harry stretches... Sits reads a bit then lays on the bench, covers his face with papers and dozes. A few minutes pass when here comes ... Mom on the scene, all breathless from having been searching for her *Son Harry...Sees this inert body on the bench with newspapers for blankets, decides it just might be Harry and gives the inert body a love tap with her umbrella!...No response gives it a firmer tap... Still no response gives it a harder love tap? While emitting a disgruntled motherly plea to wake this corpse up* " Harry!... Harry! Is that you in there? Someone told me you were here...Harry?...Answer me if that's you! Is it, is it you, son?" He's out cold, she's alongside now, moves paper from his face. "Harry it's me, your Ma!"

Harry slow to wake up and needless to say totally startled growls, ***"Stop beating on me with... with that thing, that***

umbrella! "Ma…Mom? …Whatcha doin here? ….www—
what………?
Whe-where…?"

"Come to take ya home son! Enough-a this nonsense! Look at
you sleeping on a park Bench like your half dead, with newspapers
on you ta keep you warm! Your father should see you now!"

"Mom Pop's dead!"... And Starts to go back to sleep, no
chance with his Mom here… She shakes him vigorously. "Ma
don't! Leave me be!... I ain't goin' home! I like my life here…I'm
stayin!"

She's on a roll now, shakes him harder this time, she means
business. "Nonsense son, everybody misses you, c'mon! You're
comin home with me! *NOW!"*

"Stop Ma! I don't want to go home, not now, not ever! I love
you; but I ain't goin! That's it!"

"Ya gotta! And *Right* Now! Enough's! Enough! I told you
that before. Just grab my hand! We'll get you outa here in no time
Harry!…This is no place for ya… On a park bench! What would
your sainted father think?"

"Where he is, it doesn't matter Ma!"

"But if he *were* alive, he'd be flippin mad!"

"You say Ma! But he was never was sober enough to have real
feelings for his family. You probably had to bury him with a fifth
O' Whiskey---his dying wish…Undertaker didn't even have to
embalm him!"

"Don't get smart with his memory, Son! When he ain't here to
defend himself! He was a good, hard-workin' man…So he *drank* a
little."

"A lot Ma…a lot! … Yeah he worked hard when sober, which
wasn't often."

"Well he worked when he could! Brought home every cent
  too!"

"Be honest Ma! Most went to the 3-**B's;** Booze, Bookies and Betting!...You're an angel Ma. You kept food on the table, our clothes patched and neat. But him!...You never did see his faults."

Harry agitated now gets up, stands stretches is tempted to run as far and as fast as he possibly can but dutifully, hangs in there takes his due punishment from his Mom... *Stands* faces her but is ready to run at any time, this has become a monthly ritual, and it drives him nuts...And his Ma too! But she'll never quit trying, do you blame her?"

She picks up where she left off... "I saw his faults alright, but I ignored'em, tryin' to raise you and Sis.

"How's she doin Ma?

"Good! Real good! And would love to hear from ya!... Had baby number three... You're an uncle again. Married to a good man; just made Detective... Told me to say hello, wished me luck'n gave me a 20 for you."

"I don't want *no* charity Ma! I'm happy she's doin' good. Jack's a good man. And I'm glad for her. You tried with me Ma. Even pushed me through College."

"You did that on yur own, and served in Iraq and Afghanistan too! I was proud of ya. Then you became the best English teacher at the High school, you bet!"

"Thanks Ma! Still had his genes, in my jeans. *His*!... The wild ones...You know Ma! Got hooked on Booze, Drugs! This is me!"

"This is not you! No! I refuse to believe it."

"I'm doin' Ok! Away from the pressures, the house I was trapped in, full of his memories...his shadow. I don't wanna be there no more.... I love you, wish you'd go home! I'm ok, have a few friends; doin' OK! on Rehab!"

"God Bless ya son!"

"You too Mom! Hey get this Ma I'm trying a little acting now... would you believe?"

Grabs his hand, he pulls away, she feels like dragging him home he can't keep doin this she thinks, and thinks. Tries to save him from a fate like his old man! Her voice getting shriller and shriller now, more desperate! "Forget that acting stuff son!

Life'll be different, you'll see, get a nice teaching job again. You'll be uncle Harry; get yourself a car... A girl. Life'll get better, give it a chance!"

"No!"

"Harry?" She's had it now and out of words! "Oh! Shute!... Alright!... Alright I'll go!... God bless ya son! I love ya!...I'll keep prayin' for ya! ...Never stopped!"

Walks off dejectedly, slowly almost dragging herself. She feels that low...

Now unhappy for his Mom not himself, he's happy but has separate painful emotions about all this. Guess you could call him torn. Begins to feel a little less tense now that Mom has dragged off her weary body and mind... Decides to sprawl out on Nate's special Bench once again. Pulls the newspapers over his face and slips off into an exhausted sleep.

Chapter Three

Morning in the Park

Next Morning in the Square, Nate *Leaps* up on his Bench, stretches arms toward the Sun, and greets the Sunrise, lustily! "*Arise fair Sun* *and greet the envious Moon already sick and pale with smog!* **Shine** *down warmly on this pollywog!*"

Nan up early and in a happy mood, enters his domain…
"Pollywog?... You can do better than that Nate? Or is itl
Shakespeare?... Once again It's your fair Annie interrupting your
soliloquy, your moment…But Mr. Bard I come with a message
from His Honor the Mayor, who thought he might be imposing
upon your private space to just pop in and make an urgent
request."

"And didn't have the temerity to do it himself, is that it?"

He adds Facetiously, "I guess he just wanted to show you he
did things in a politically correct way."

"Said, he was tied up at City Hall, and thought that since you
and I are friends, that I wouldn't mind relaying a message!"

"Sooo tactful! Resorts to spying and phone calls; is there no
justice?"

Nan in her worst *Lower Eastside Accent,* "So dramatic you are!
Listen Mr. Bard with me I'm easy and listed in the phone book.
Having little regard for Security!"

"Et tu Nan, my dear friend, inserting just one more thrust of
the dagger into my bony, starved body."

Still with the *accent*, "First Romeo, now Caesar? So privileged
I am to be in your company !"… Back to normal Nan, "Step
down out of the limelight and let me tell you what he said. Then
we can part company my bold but corny Nate!"

"Now it sounds like you're doing *Taming of the Screw!"*
"Shrew!... Actually, *I thought,* I was pretty good."

"You weren't bad… But back to the business at hand he
requests you meet with Senator Hildy Brodrik Minton. She has
some important issues to ask your advice on; but can only meet
you at night. What do you say to that?"

"I don't know that I care for her politics, but I can *straighten*
her out on a few issues… If it's night time she requests; it's night
time she'll get at my abode in 'The WAS,' by the light of my one
Bare bulb and a dozen flickering candles."

She's quick, "As long as the *Bulb* is bare and not you! I'll convey your message. He also said, *she'd* call back later today; and asked if you'd like a snack?"

"Yes! Yes!... 'My kingdom for a Snack!' They know what I like... Tell'em tomorrow night! Nan, if you will?"

"Now you're Henry the Fifth, you're amazing!... Tomorrow night it is!" ... Very warmly now because she loves this enigmatic madman. "See you later!... Hope you don't get to be a celebrity. As it is, you're getting to be even more withdrawn and not your usual lovable self. ...Don't even seem to have time for me anymore."

"I'll always have time for you my beautiful Nan... And now for the matter at hand if this means free Roast Beef Sandwiches.

Bring'em on!... I'm beginning to enjoy my role as Oracle, too bad I don't have Apollo's Delphic Temple to hold meetings in. But I've got the next best thing, 'The WAS !' Thanks! See ya later. Got some catchin' up to do... Got a windfall of papers need reading, got my work cut out for me. Anything comes up, you know where to find me."

"Not even a little hug?"

Nate condescends, gives her a *little hug*...... there!"

"No wonder your first wife divorced you!... See you later Lover!" Leaves quickly, feeling rejected, disappointed, this guy she likes isn't easy. But loves him with all his faults, appearance and aromas... Only a *mother lion* could appreciate.

Nate now exhilarated, happy that perhaps now after all these years will again be appreciated by the world for his knowledge his genius, his prowess!... Suddenly, jumps to his

51

feet, stretches catlike to the warm Sun; then sits , crosses his legs, reads a few sentences, smiles, to himself, to the World pleased with himself. Salutes with his cupa cold-coffee, his *'Brown Nectar of Life!'*

Evensong

Next evening, the lighting dim with bare bulb and candles in his abode. Furnished in 60's Flowerchild motif with once white-plastic lawn chairs standing centurion like guarding Nate's famed Abode. Its Décor referred to by Friends as a 60's Late Hovel... His ears perk up to the sound of footsteps coming up the long winding staircase. Now alive with audible mutterings of the Senator, breathless after the climb enters carrying food and coffee.

Energetically, smilingly, but still a breathless after those steep steps in the musty Arch... Manages a warm greeting. " Aah and you must be Nate of Washington Arch Square, fame. Glad to meet you! I'm Senator Hildy Brodrik Minton... Who else would be mad enough to climb up all those steps... Call me Hildy!"

Nate carefully rises from his antiquated Flower-Child Throne like, plastic chair, as befits The Oracle of Was. He greets her, like the Monarch he feels he is and their equal. "Welcome to my humble abode compliments of the Taxpayers of New York. And borrowed from the Rodents that once inhabited it." She smilingly offers her hand which he takes and gently shakes.

"Greetings from myself Hildy, and your Mayor who sends his regards." He vigorously Shakes her hand. Then offers her one of his more regal chairs with a higher more elegant, filigreed plastic back... *They* sit and smile at each other waiting for the other to start. Nate decides to break the ice. " Even though I may not always agree with your politics, Hildy Dear. It's a pleasure to meet and greet you in my humble hovel."

"Humble but cozy with a distinguished 5th Ave address! My pleasure too...The Mayor couldn't say enough good things about you, Nate... Your Pulitzer Prize, the D.C. Think Tank, even favors the theory that just perhaps you predicted 911, but no one listened at the time. A fine Professor. Even compared you to Plato and Aristotle. He feels you're a genuine Oracle! Capable of predicting the future--- and wise... *As* some of my Jewish constituency might say ...Ah regular Solomon you are!"

"Not the first time I've been called that. But if it'll put you at ease, I've been called a lot worse... Hildy ya gotta admit it's a little bit strange you not coming with Security. And ... a snack?"

"Not to worry! Security is discreetly downstairs. I didn't want to alarm an Oracle for heaven's sake! ... Though you may not tell me what I *want* to hear. As to your snack I want you to know we spared no expense or effort to purchase your snack from one of the finest Deli's on 7th Ave., with kosher pickle, which is my favorite too... *Enjoy!"* She happily hands it to him.

"Thank you!"... Takes it, opens the bag inhales it for the longest time, takes a couple of bites out of it. "Sorry Hildy it just smelled so good!" ...

"Glad to see you're enjoying it so very much."

"Oh yeah, thanks! It's choice, like filet minion to me... Now back to business. I may not tell you what you *want* to hear, but it'll be the *truth!"*

"You're welcome, and for the record; truth is what I'm after. Incidentally I hear tell you've got a Doctorate and a Pulitzer?

"Yes!"

"That's it you don't wish to elaborate?... *Well!* What a pedigree!"

"For a Mutt!... No need it's not like your writing my
   Biography."

"My but your self-effacing! I like that!... Your humility."

"Hildy to be honest, I'm a private, opinionated, and a
sometimes humble guy. I just know what my achievements have
been and from where I sit there's no need to advertise, they're on
the public record. And as usual, it's been this way most of my
adult life. And as you've already sensed women see right through
me."

"What's this I hear about you refusing to make permanent
ties?"

Almost falls out of his chair!... " Is there anything your spies
didn't find out about me? I have nothing to offer a woman, so why
waste her time. Tell your spies that even if it sounds boring, it's
because I'm the most Boring person I know!... That's how I like's
to keep it!... Thank you!"

"You're far from boring and you know it. The fact of the
matter is you demean my troops who hate the Spy label and who
prefer to be called investigative reporters. But they *are* good aren't
they? But expensive!"

"Hey it's only Taxpayer money!"

"Well spoken, a tad if I may say it offensive but honest. I like
you Nate, you're straightforward, and honest, wish you were on
my team … But down to business, though I find you fascinating;
I'd like to stay and chat but I'm on a mission, so I'll get to the
point with a loaded, double barreled question… **Should I** run for
office in the next election; and if I do; what are my chances?"

"I like that in a politician, and a woman. Ya don't mince
words. But that, dear Hildy is a tough, *Double Barreled* 12 guage
question! Not easy to address… and one which requires
consultation."

"*You?*… Have a consulting staff?"

"No, but frequently confer with my friend Alex."

"Alex?"

"*Alexander!*

She getting a little annoyed, " Nate stop playing name games! …

"Who Alexander…?"

"I thought the Mayor and just perhaps your *Spies* told you about my ethereal friends?"

"Not a word!"

"Well then, the honorable Alexander Hamilton, himself !"

"Thee--- Alexander Hamilton!?… You *do* run with Extinguished company!"

"I do, don't I?"

"Two Questions, have you been friends long? And doesn't your friendship seem a bit strange?"

" *Nah!*… I met Alex soon after I moved here. Apparently he was lonely for companionship and curious to find out who had the audacity to move into his space. … Personally I don't see anything strange in commiserating with astral beings, the ones that go bump in the night and sometimes ride ghostly white stallions in a soundless gallop through Washington Square and the Park."

"Then you've been friends since then."

"At first merely acquaintances, but then it developed into a great friendship. Because he was lonely and being an ambitious man whose life was snuffed away at an early age, and not as well liked as some would believe… In fact after the Revolution hoped to be The General in charge of the First, Peacetime American Army. Which unfortunately never came to fruition."

"Didn't realize that" Hildy responds, "Though I'm aware he was a very ambitious."

"He's had plenty of time to stew over that matter after being dead all this time, ever since Burr had the audacity to kill him in their duel in Weehawken, New Jersey."

"Is it true that he didn't even attempt to get off a shot at Aaron…" Hildy recalls, "Almost as if he had a death wish."

"Hmm, hmm… So the story goes… He did mention also that after being shot he was taken to his home near here; mortally wounded, and died the next day… Been wandering round 'The Was' ever since. His spirit just can't find peace!... And likes to commute by Subway from Trinity Cemetery, downtown where he was buried because it's near to where he used to live, quite frankly stated that he loves this park which happens to be the location of an old potter's field, where the buried poor folk and yellow fever victims and where there's lots of ghostly happenings ongoing here that he enjoys…. And we both enjoy talking about the state of the nation. He's brilliant, graduated Kings College which is now Columbia, and where I taught for many years."

"You do tell fascinating and very Interesting tales!... Though, frankly you do seem a tad delusional? But manage to travel in excellent company, even if not of this world…. Now … I have a serious question, for you."

"Fire away! Though you think me delusional, my supernatural friends *are* real!"

"Never doubted it for a minute!... Now then Mr. Oracle I'd like your views on how to put an end to the flow of weapons over the U.S. border into Mexico and the hands of Drug Cartels?"

"A tough task that I've given a lot of thought to, and for which I have a possible solution!... Because the situation grows worse by the day!… For starters my suggestion on the matter is to make a pact with China!"

"With China!?... You are delusional!"

"Perhaps, but remember how the British sold The London Bridge, to an American Millionaire years ago? Sent it over here, all parts numbered and *Reassembled*, out West."

"Yes! *Yes!* And I was mortified!"

"Me too!... My *point* is this Senator--- the *Great Wall of China*, is 4163 Miles long. Too costly for China to maintain! All we need is half of it, say 2081.5 miles ... Purchased at a reasonable price of course! Which we'll make appetizing by offering to use Chinese expertise to advise us on its *Re-assembly.* They'll be more than happy to unload it!"

"You think? ... But how do we get it here?"

"*Disassemble it!...* Number the parts, ship it to the U.S. Then Ta Da! *Reassemble* it on the border between the U.S. and Mexico. As a joint project, using American, Mexican and Chinese talent, workers, and engineers!"

"But how's this going to put an end to the weapon crisis?

"By allowing the U.S. and Mexico to better control the activities of Weapon Smugglers at prime entry points on the Border. Thereby preventing Drug Lords from continuing the illegal flow of weapons from the U.S. into the hands of criminals."

"And you actually think this is a good plan?"

"Gotta be! Then make it politically correct; by making it Ecologically correct with flower and vegetable gardens planted at its base on either side; adding beauty; and food to the tables of the hungry on both sides of the wall."

"Next thing you'll tell me, it'll be a tourist attraction."

"You're reading my mind, Hildy! Tourists from all over the world will come to visit The Great Wall of China on the Mexican, American border. Bringing prosperity to both and make it easier for both peoples to travel freely but safely."

"And you honestly think that China will be willing to part with her Historic Wall?

"Sure ---we're only purchasing *Half* the Wall here!... Leaving half to China for *their* tourist trade. It's an Environmentally- Green- Goodwill and prosperous Gesture! One that'll extend coast to coast. There it is then my solution in a nut shell!"

"That *is* Genius! And Innovative! But obviously needs some thought.   And all predicated on the world not taking me for DELUSIONAL… or in a word, *NUTS!"*

"It's 'Out of the Box' thinking!"

" *Sure* is! Meanwhile I'm beginning to doubt the Mayor's ability to recognize an Oracle."

"Hildy I'm sorry… I didn't volunteer for this duty and if you want your sandwich back, here it is!" Reluctantly offers it to her.

"I'm sorry!... I have this tendency to be *Blunt!*... Ruffle peoples feathers. You're right to get upset. Don't be silly the sandwich is yours. And if you can get some answers from Alex. I'd be deeply appreciative. *Oh My!*... I'm beginning to sound and think like you!"

"I have that affect on people!"

"Gotta warn you I have no influence over the outcome."

"Understood and I don't expect you to doctor the results. After all this isn't The West Village Version of *"Water Gate!"* Besides I've got a tough skin and will run for office; even if he or anybody else says: '*Figet* about it Lady!' (Clowns around with her worst version of mafia *street talk… she thinks.)* We don't want no womin runnin dis here country Lady! Go home to your family, clean, do laundry, shop, get your kids to school on time that's what all women should do! It's in the Kitchen and bedroom wit youse!... And Oh yeah! *Keep dem home-fires burning wit-out burning da house down!"*

" *Why* Hildy that was a damned good you sounded just like a Hood from the lower Eastside.!"

"Actually I heard that yelled at me more than once!"

"I can believe it!"

"Remember now! All kidding aside! I need more input from Alex on this weapon crisis!"

"You bet!... I'll let you know as soon as Alex pays me a call. Got a feeling he might show up tonight. He's long overdue and might drop in to get out of the damp weather; says it's tough on his phantom pain from his old gut wound... But Wait! *Wait!* I have to be honest with you Hil! If we are to continue in this collaboration there's something you should know about me."

"Well?"

"In case it should ever come up and your associates need to know more about me."

"Yes?"

"The reason why I split from society the reason is............"

"Yes?"

"To escape!"

"To escape?"

"Yes!...The 3 P's!" ...

"The 3 P's?" ....

"*Yes!*... Politics, Pundits, and Politicians!"

"Sorry! About that but we found you; so the reality of this scenario is you're stuck with us."

"Aah!... Point well taken. I'll do my best for you Hil, even though you're a *Politician!"*

"That's all I ask, thank you!... Alright then, I'll expect to hear from you as soon as you find out something. Tell Alex I think he would have made a fine president, and his wife Elizabeth, a great first lady. I'll bet *She* never did any housekeeping!"... Starts to leave, takes a moment, gives him a warm smile, and hug *(she likes him)* then leaves.

   Nate does not stand on ceremony when it comes to a Roast beef sandwich, especially if it has a pickle in the middle… Hungrily attacks it sandwich, dill and all!… Then with great pleasure and ecstasy gulps down the still warm coffee… Senses something; quickly whirls sees Alex; whom no one else to his knowledge has ever been privileged to see or hear. Does this make him *Mad? Delusional?* Or Simply Privileged and Paranormal?

Chapter Four

Alexander Hamilton Drifts in!

"That you? Alex... Whew!

Sure startled me! Think by now I'd be used to you popping in unannounced like this... Hungry?... What am I saying? I forgot you don't do food! Are *you alright?* You're looking paler than usual. Here rest your aching spirit on this chair, still warm from my visit with the Senator... Not impressed I see? *Oh! It's not that?... She seems too edgy, ambitious and a woman!...* Aah!... But things have *changed* since you passed in 1804! .... I'm sorry I hadn't noticed you watching us from the shadows. Or I might have introduced you to the Senator! What am I saying? I'm forgetting that she wouldn't be able to see or hear you... Alex allow me to put to you a few questions from the Senator she would appreciate your opinion on.   Do you think, she should run for office? If so will she be elected?... *Hmm, hmm!... Too hard even for you and your underground sources to predict.* I see!... You're beginning to sound like a politician? *Aah! Shaking your head are you?...* You don't think so! I see! How do I break the news?.....What?... *Just tell her outright!...* Well--- if I have to?.......   Now this very key and important question ---What about my idea of bringing over Half of the Great Wall of China?... Why that expression on you face?... A *Clever idea but the Chinese will never go for it...* Well I'm not surprised *you* wouldn't go for it... It's too surreal a scheme for a distinguished General like yourself........So much for my pull with important people in Low Places... Alex I'm detecting a certain hostility you're not your usual friendly self, and seem edgy... *Oh the phantom pain from the Duel is acting up...*Try ice!... All right! No need to get testy! ... Aah... I know that look you need to get going! Aah, *Gotta Spirit Committee Meeting!* Thanks for the input... Feel better! See you later! Salutes him, plops down in his throne and goes back to reading and eating. Wow I wish they'd put a much brighter light bulb in this place!

The Next Morning at Sunrise, Nate, Mary, Harry, *are facing East to greet it---As they raise their arms and chant loudly.*

"Arise fair Sun, and greet the envious Moon, already in pale Smoggy-Ruin!" Then--- *Briefly Sing a few bars... Good morning Sunshine! All Hail another new Day!"*

Nan belatedly enters from West 4[t.h]St., speaking as she rambles over. "What have we here, a traveling troupe of *troubled* Troubadours?"

"Join us Nan as we Salute Our Maker and the Sun!"

Nan feeling silly, being more inhibited than the rest hesitatingly joins them as they raise their arms, again... A daily ritual, on Sunny days.

Mary naturally irritated when Nan is around has to open her big mouth, she's honest, figures has every right to do so. "I was having a good time till miss snooty came along!"

"Nan enjoys fun like you Mar; no need to get an attitude!"

"If I need to have an attitude I will that's my right. And yeah and I want the world to know I'm jealous, so there! And have a right to be... She *likes* you, but I *love* you, and that's that!"

"Not to worry Mary, Nate has no ties and that's that!"

"Speaking of ties. You'd love to get your manicured, perfumed hands on him, to convert him to a snob in a *suit!* I don't care what *you* want! I love him for what he is! Not what he wuz! An' *I* don't like you hangin' round him, all the damn time!"

"We're all friends here Mary. Contrary to what you think; I don't have to hang around him, he knows my virtues. And there's no cause for animosity, it ruins the Yin and the Yang!

"Virtues? Ha!... An' I got your YinYang!" Screams it as she assails *Nan and gives her a good hard shove!* "There's your Yin!" *Shoves her harder this time.* "And your Yang!"

Nan, surprised, defends herself with a quick shove, but too late. "Take that you, you trollop!"

"Rich Bitch, have another Yang!

Nan now showing another side of her; yanks Mary's hair.

"There take that! *Cheeze!* You have yucky, greasy, dirty hair! Grubby street Bitch!"

"OOWWW!... Oh so now I'm the Bitch? If I'm a Bitch," I'll have a piece of your dyed, *I spied* --- gray roots *hair* ... Tootsie!"

As she *grabs a hunk of Nan's hair,* There that looks more like how a Bitch should look--- au naturelle!

"Oh! Oh! Ooooh!…You! You!… groveling, grubby, sewer whore! *(Who-a)*"

Finally not able to take all this female angst and carnage, Nate steps in and grabs Nan; While Harry grabs Mary; in an attempt at breaking it up.

Nate now *Irate,* "Ladies! Ladies! Break it up , we're all friends here!"

Mary screams, "Hey I ain't no Lady, remember that! I'm Mary Street urchin, derelict and former junkie at your service! Aaand Let go-a me Harry!... *I'll* fix her hair good, so's her Ritzy friends'll call her Baldeeee!...*Baldeee!"* As *Harry with all his strength continues to holds her; and she begins to chill out!.*

Nan outa control now and angry as Hell; let's out a yell that curls Mary's greasy locks!>>> "Let me at her Nate!…I'll fix her hair so they'll have to put it in a cast!"... Nan suddenly stops looks down at herself as she begins to shutter from rage, what has she come to anyway? She's never, ever been this angry before and starts laughing her silly, angry head off till she's totally consumed, convulsed in laughter and comforts her own being with, " what the Hell everybody I've just experienced a case of unholy angst! … What a jolt! I've never been this angry before…Why if I had a gun I would've shot her or a guillotine I woulda have chopped her greasy head off! Crazy Huh? Starts *Laughing hysterically, still seething but easing off.* "Her hair in a cast! Ah! Ha ha ha ha ha!"

This relieves the tension a bit. And they all bust out *laughing!*

"Ladies! Ladies! Is this anyway to behave? Please, let's all love each other as friends, with no animosity! Time now to restore the Yin and the Yang!… Ok Girls?" Neither responds…Ok Girls?

Nate and Harry tentatively release them; then have to grab them again!

Mary still out of a control. "Never!...Never!...No YinYang! Never! Not for me!"

Harry beginning to lose his cool now, "Cool it Mary! Before we wake the dead and someone calls 911 and the police arrive!"

"Yeah!" Nate says, "We're not exactly on their heartfelt best friends list!"

"You can say that again!" Harry knows this from his own personal experience.

" Come'on Mary! I'm willing! I'll meet you half way, what do ya say? I'll Yin! If you'll...

" Nooo!.... Never!... Neva...Well......" slowly coming around thinking it over carefully... " Weeelll... If I gotta.... I gotta!......Alright...I'll Yang!"

"That's more like it!" Nate philosophically adds, "We're family and families are the most and toughest arguers and pugilists!"

Mary quizzes Nate... uummm..."does that mean they fight a lot?"

"Worse than that Mar, worse than that!"

"Alright then!" Harry happily announces, "Way to go!...We're all *fiends* again! Uuuur friends!"

"Right!" Mary begrudgingly... "Alright, I'll try to get along." Harry finally but with uncertainty releases her.

"Nan agrees," "Me too!"... Errr... "Will try?"

Nate feels it's safe now to unleash Nan. " I'd invite you all to breakfast, except I'm short-a-cash, and would be embarrassed to walk into a swank fast food joint... Howeva' I'll share this large bagel... Harry your trusty plastic knife if you please, to cut this delicacy into 4 equal pieces!" *Harry deftly hands him his treasured knife. As Nate takes over the sensitive allocating of a bagel, after carefully cutting it, hands out the pieces.* "Now we'll all drink from the *Peace* cup, which Nan has generously provided, with fresh hot coffee." Which they now pass around with exaggerated sensitivity.

Nan says, "I'll pass!... I've had breakfast."

"Whuzza matter?" Mary pries, "you fraid-a catching our germs, miss Prim?"

"No way, I just thought...Oh never mind. Harry hand me that...Damn!...Peace cup! *She noisily takes a huge gulp.* Umm good! Hands it to Mar, "there wise guy!"

"That wasn't so hard!" Nate admonishes, "and this is just a little ceremony to our Maker, for his Sunshine, to show respect, and to keep the Peace!"

" I wasn't trying to be an irreverent party poop here!" Nan pleads.

"Just a pain in the ass Party Poop!" Mary jabs, "Which you are ... You don't even need ta try!... And *you* with the Mansions and the money don't need Nate!... But *I Do!"*

"Mary I like everybody...even you, and have as much right to be here and share the Sunrise and the bagel! Right Nate? *He spares her a nod...* "Let's strive for Harmony and enjoy the moment! *As she Breaks into a warm, open, friendly generous, smile and healthy laughter!"*

Which they ALL join in on.

"Alright! I guess ya can't have what ya can't have!" Mary *not* quite giving up the battle, *"For* the time being!"

" Is that a Yogi-Berra-ism?" Nate slips in...

"*I* said it!... And me--- *Mary!* Can out Yogi, him or any other Yokel!"

"Spoken like a true feminist." The Oracle announces then asks, "What's everybody doing today?"

"After breakfast," Harry announces, "I thought I'd stroll over to the library and research my new book: *'The Narcissus Complex in Derelicts.' –Or- 'The Id in Every Skid.* That'll take up most of my day. That and reading the tabloids about the never ending mess in Middle East... Mary if you'd care to join me?"

Mary the born actress in her very best Posh British accent replies, "Aftah today's fracas I'll certainly need ta take my mind off-a-things.... Dear Harry, I'd be delighted, for I've got research ta do on my new thriller; tha *'Nicotine Factor' or 'How My Life Went Up In Smoke!'* A killah of a book and a sure best-sella. Tha last you'll evuh read!... Alive! Hee-Haaaa!

"I wish I could go," Nan says, " but I'm stuck waiting for a call from our political friends, who want to *confer* with Nate."

"Meanwhile your old Professor is researching Afghanistan with its rich History of devastation and exploitation by Genghis Khan, the English, Russians, and Taliban! And is now most widely known for its Poppy growing and the Taliban. If you want me ... I'll be here in the Sun. On *my* bench; compliments of the taxpayers, to whom I say thank you!... So *Alas!* Parting is such sweet sorrow, never mind that!... I'll see you all tomorrow... at Sunrise!" Then grandly Sits, crosses legs, reads, drinks his beloved coffee.

While Harry and Mary Leave arm in arm like a couple of swells. " Till the MORROW! Nate!"

"The *MORROW!*"

"Meanwhile your Nan has a question for you Nate Dear. Something which has been on my mind for awhile. And which that YinYang fiasco brought to a head? "

"Certainly! But if you would please madam follow Nate the Pied Piper"... He starts toward "The WAS" as he *mimes* the playing of a flute. And she obediently follows, him to the Arch!

" I picked a fine day for a talk, but please let's not argue!"

" I Promise! My time is yours."

" Not really; those are just words, you don't share things with me like you used to."

" Sorry! I'll do my best to improve... A few more steps and we'll be in the sanctity of my pad." They enter together and walk up the dank, winding Stairway to his penthouse in the Park as he sometimes refers to it, and they sit. "Can I offer you anything; a half a container of cold coffee, a cigar butt?"

"Please dear Nate try to be serious!"

"Cancel the cigar butt!"

"Will you get serious!"

"And the cold coffee!"

"You're infuriating!... At the risk of being obsessive; I need to ask you something?"

"Shoot!"

"Will you, damn it! Come live with me!... I love you!... Would fight to the death for you! Pull out Mary's hair for you!... Don't care about your past. *Just you!*... Nate we could have an exciting life together. Even Travel!... If you don't want to work; *Fine!*... I have wealth, you... you could be my lover, my adviser. Let me take you away from all of this... this Depravity!"

"You forgot squalor! But I *love* this...this Depravity! And Squalor! ... But *No* thanks!... This may sound nuts! But I enjoy this life, no cares, no responsibility, fine friends, communing with nature, strolls in the park, the ongoing people show!... Here I'm friends with the world... *Everybody* respects me for being a *nobody*... I'm happy!"

"*Happy?*... Sappy is more like it! Nate! I've always been Frank with you simply because I love you! And promise not to give up on us!"

"We've always had a good relationship and friendship!"

She rebuts him, viciously-facetiously *with*, *"how* can you consider our relationship, merely friendship...Wow! You're a hard case! Thanks for that *my friend!... Nan's not giving up easily and being known for her quick thinking which she employs on old Nate the lucky recipient as she swings into a new strategy...* " I *know,* let's go to a museum. You pick! We could go to MOMA, or the Met, or take the train up to Beacon on the Hudson and check out the DIA, the latest rage.... Com'on Nate, lighten up! We'll start at my place where you can take a *quick* shower, so you get used to the feel of water and soap again. You know like spiff up a little at a time.... Don't want to upset your Eco-System. Later go to a quaint restaurant; nuthin' fancy, just good food, ambiance, service... A good wine list... Just the *two* of us... Nate please me this once! You can always come back to your security blanket-- 'The WAS.'... We'll have a grand time! And the good news is; I can outfit you with the clothes of my dead husband. He wouldn't mind!"

"But I would! And **HE** would if he knew you were consorting with a known vagrant... *Look!* I'm happy sittin,' watchin' the grass grow, pan handlers, pan, listenin' to the pigeons coo!.... Reading about what's goin' on in this crazy world of ours, all the time trying to figure if Armageddon is here or about to happen?"

"Well is it?"

"Any Day now!"

"Do tell! Oh! and by the way you forgot--- *Hear the crows, crow!* But never mind me! I'll go!... Get out of your hair; and let you know if anyone calls." *She kisses him lightly but then, almost instantaneously her whole being igniting with anger spews!* "Waaaiiit a minute! ...Damn it! You're not getting off the hook that easy. Oh no! Let me tell you something!... This has been building for a long time!... Number One! I'm sick and tired of these rotten, dirty, smelly clothes," *as she grabs his shirt ripping his holey Brooks Brothers shirt off his back.* "You wanna know something ? I can't stand'em!... Sooo I'll just have

69

to rip'em all off you! … I've had enough of your filthy Ways… I love you; damn it! But--- don't ask me why!"

" Nan Stop! Will you! Don't do this you're ruining my best outfit!"

"You mean these Rags! Rags!! You've gotta be kidding!

I can't stop now I'm mad as hell and not done tearing these rotten clothes off!" … *As she continues to rip away with malice of forethought!* And I'm not going to take it anymore! Damn! *Rip! Rip!* Damn! *Tear! Tear! Rip!*... Damn! Damn! Rip! Damn!

Nate starts laughing hysterically then nervously, hesitatingly, thinks she's in a vicious mood, never seen her like this before… Hell NO! finally gets up enough nerve to *protest*... "What are you doing?…I love these old rags, uuh… clothes, they're comfortable, broken in, vented with holes for year round wear. Perfect for all occasions, with an aroma of the great outdoors!" … She Continues ripping away in spite of his protesting because now--- finally, he defends his clothes …without hurting her of course that's not his way. … Stop Nan!... *Too much caffeine?...* What's become of you?... You've gone bonkers! First with Mary; now me. What a tiger! … Hmm… *Now he has second thoughts… begins to feel his old Virile, young-blood self. Kinda likes that in a woman… Attacking my clothes; ripping 'em off my back! Imagine that? Finds his voice,* "Back off sweetie, before you destroy my entire wardrobe!"

Breathing hard now she mutters under her fiery, exhausted breath. " I can't stand you like this; an educated genius looking and smelling like a Bum! I'm offering you a lifeline… *take it Nate!* Climb on board! You can't continue like this, you can't!" *She's had it, and finally breaks down, and cries.*

This is unlike Nate here but he succumbs to her truth, her emotions. Hey let's face it! Her love for him and would you believe *caresses* her... "Come on Nan! There's nothin' you can do! This is my life! *Finds himself dragging out these words to make his point. "* I'm happy!...HAPPEEE!... I've been out *thherrre.* I know what it's liiike; that's why I'm *here!* I'm doin' alright. Sorry you fell for this old Bum, but it wasn't my fault and"...

"Oh! Now you're gonna tell me it's my doing? That I'm vulnerable since my John died, maybe, but that's the way it is... I won't stifle my feelings for you. I don't care what you say; nor how you smell ...Wait just a minute here... I take that back... Yes I do care how you smell, what's wrong with that anyway?... Aaah shoot! Just forget I ever acted this way! And be your smelly, go lucky...crazy self." *She grabs a handkerchief out of her Coach Bag and exits crying.*

"Bye Nan!" *Gives her a cursory wave. He's an enigma.* Getting over the emotion of the scene but nevertheless affected and moved by it, manages quickly to devolve back to his protective Id as a Skid *not meant to rhyme here but what the Hell!* Quickly decides to read for awhile, not to be cold about it but after all her visit interrupted his busy schedule... Then unexpectedly quietly, you could say deliberately, clandestinely Alex and a Ghostly friend, pop-in! These visitations are reserved for Alex and *No* one else sees or hears them. And you can be sure prefer it that way. Nate notices them drift in, is happy to see both ghostly apparitions greeting them warmly. Always encouraging them to drop by and is never too busy to spend time with them. After all it's always a joy to him when they visit and usually very informative though *Eerie!... Very Eerie!*

 * "Good Day Alex!... It's about time I greeted my Ghostly friends. What a pleasure seeing you at this early hour! Who's your friend?" *Aah!... John.* "Sorry, I shoulda recognized the

71

Barrymore profile!… What brings you round?" … *I see the Sun warms your Spirit!* " And John?… *You feel the same*… wish you could move back to your place on West 4ᵗʰ" …. No *Sorry!* I don't have any Scotch!……. *Sooo!* I heard from some of the *Spirits,* once actors who were buried here in Potters field that you had finally confessed to them in an orgy of penance, trying to cleanse your soul of your once, serious drinking habit causing you to admit to them that it was a crazy scheme to make your Penthouse into The Garden of Eden, putting tons of topsoil, exotic plants and trees on your nice, old land-lady's roof!… Sure ticked her off and the inspectors who condemned her place till it was removed! Nothing serious, just that the building started caving-in and oozing mud!… Anyway enough about the good old days… *Glad* you both dropped by" …… *"Nooo!* I haven't seen the Senator. I expect I'll be hearing from her through Nan. Nothin's gonna stop Hildy! After all, bein' married to Mister popularity---President Wild Phil Minton, left her stronger!... Where you off ? Aaaah!……. I'm disappointed you can't stay and chat a bit longer. John you to tell me about those wild experiences you had in Show Biz, and Alex about those heated exchanges you had with old John Adams about making you the Commanding General of the new Peacetime Army" …….*Alright then!* Another time when you have more time….. "Good! See you then… Enjoy your stroll round the park!" *Watches them leave,* then goes back to reading.

Harry *storms in,* "Nate Hi! Seen Mary? …We were supposed to have lunch at the food kitchen, this is Chili day. We both likes our Chili. Said she'd meet me here."

Nate awakened from his reverie and reading is suddenly jarred back into his world. "Haven't seen her… Pull up a chair; grab some newsprint and stay awhile! If you can spare the time, gets kinda lonely in here from time to time.

Sits next to Nate reads, who puts his paper down. " I'm too edgy! Gotta get goin' or they'll close the kitchen before I get there.

Might run outa Chili, and they make a damn good chili, throw everything good into it, real tasty , even had an old dishrag by mistake once with turnips painted on it kinda added to the flavor, it did... Just tell her to meet me there will ya!"

"You bet!... Bring me some rolls will ya...!

"See what I can do. How about dessert, saltines with deli-jelly?"

"Make it Strawberry that's my favorite!... See you later."

"Right!" *Harry rushes out can't miss out on that Chili!*

A few minutes pass when Nan scurries in announcing... "Great News! The Senator called and wants another meeting with the now famous Oracle. She figured about eight tonight, I said that's a good time, but I'll call back to confirm."

"Cuts into my Prime TV Show time."

"I know you're kidding by the cute little way your mouth curls up at the corners, and your unshaven face turns red with animated glee but in case you haven't noticed you have no TV! And I do if you're interested?"

"I'm impressed but could care less with all the dribble that appears on TV nowadays. At least so I've heard."

"For once I can agree with you. Our minds are in agreement on many things why we would make a wonderful *married* couple."

"You!... You are astute! But not always on the mark with that comment but I *like* you just the same."

"Thanks for that Mr. Generosity!... So, I'll get back to her and let her know, it's a go. And by the way *Lover* you may want to clean your *specious* apartment. Since it's the maid's day off."

" Great idea! I may even throw saw dust around for ambiance."

"Like Mc Sorley's Bar!... Your Notoriety is getting hard for me to handle!"

"It's my Persona, it attracts all types, even politicians!"

As she starts to exit... "I'll drop by after you've spoken to Hildy. Is that what she likes you to call her? I'm beginning to feel twangs of jealousy. I think she's got a crush on your Musk! Bye lover!"

Mr. homebody actually begins to sweep with an almost straw-less straw broom, throws, dirt and junk in a plastic bag, lights candles, rolls up his bedroll, turns on his scratchy but functional FM Radio to classical, hums... feigns exhaustion from that minimal volume of work. Decides this is too much exertion for one day, sits down, relaxes and cogitates then as if to stimulate his senses starts reading the Wall street journal, to see where he might invest his money if he had any ... A disdainful thought to him, but he carries on bravely. Awaits quietly as he relaxes in his chair, to read, to absorb! *Thinks aloud! Damn, I love my life!'*

A few minutes go by and in pops Mary. not too delicately looking for Harry. "Nate!... Nate!"...... When he concentrates the Arch could collapse around him and he wouldn't know it! So thoroughly engrossed in his reading is he. "For Heaven's sake Nate I'm trying to reach you... Hello in there--- this is Mary calling Nate Oracle of Was from Planet Earth to find out if you have seen Harry?... Seems I've lost him!...... Come in Nate!... I was supposed to go to the Food Kitchen with him for Chili, but I'm runnin late Nate! You seen him? He was gonna meet me here."

Finally Comes out of his stupor! "Oh Mar! When did you come in? ...err you missed Harry?...ooh, oh sure, Harry...Yeah! Oh that- Harry uuum... Yes Harry was here lookin for you. Saw you were late, got cold feet; afraid the Food Kitchen would close and was hot for his Chili! Ha! ...Hot for his Chili!"... *(always laughs at his small jokes.)*

"Not funny Nate!... Why, that dog! Some friend. You can tell his stomach means more to him than our friendship. Maybe I can still make it. I'll bring you a bun. Gotta run!" She's outa there!

74

Nate shakes his head in disbelief... what was that?
Sighs "Oh Well!" calmly gets back to *his reading,*

Chapter Five

Senator Hildy

Evening and Nate, quite content hanging out in his abode, still reading by quaint candlelight and bare bulb. Awaits Hildy his brusque Senator friend due any minute. When --- like a Starburst of Fireworks with accompanying explosions who should arrive... 'But Herself'... Calling out, loudly from the stairs. "Nate! It's me, Hildy, right on time and just in time to prevent you from starving, bringing my effervescent self along with a two-snack surprise! One for now, and one for breakfast." Enters energetically. "Look at you! Why you're a regular *News* junkie!"

"Yes! Yes!... I try to keep up with the *Chaos* in the world, the Riots and Armageddon in the Middle East!... Greetings Senator, you look *Well!*... Welcome to my humble flat which I cleaned diligently knowing you were coming."

"It sparkles, with a subdued, damp, mildewed green luminescence! Good to see you again, I enjoy your vibrancy, your, Joie de Vivre! Relaxed, *sits, crosses her legs... Totally at home.*

"Yes my decorator is fond of that Hue! Ah I like that you like those traits in me. Hope you'll feel the same after I tell you what Alex said about your running for office.

"Not to worry. See this exterior it's actually a suit of armor! And safe against any news good or bad you happen to bring me."

"First I have to tell you, Alex is not your biggest fan; secondly, he doesn't think you stand a very good chance of winning."

"Why am I not surprised, Mr. Hamilton was outspoken when alive; now dead, even bolder, probably a chauvinist! Tell him he's got nothing to fear, from me!

"Outspoken; but a chauvinist? Not my Dear *Spirit* friend Alex!

"Nevertheless, I will run as a candidate in the primary... *Win!* that, and the election. My ultimate goal become the first female president of the U.S."

"Promise you'll never become involved with any of the young male interns?"

"Promise! Besides I don't smoke *cigars!"*

"Aah!... And on that importing of the China Wall idea; *He cynically* called it a highly creative scheme! But didn't think the Chinese would go for it."

"That figures!... Anyway, enjoy your snacks Nate here they are, still a little warm. Thanks for checking with your underground on those things. Can't say I'm surprised at anything *he* said! Now I have to run! Been a pleasure meeting you... Don't know when we'll meet again."

" My pleasure too! Sorry you're leaving so soon. Come whenever you care to. I'm at your service, though you may not always want to hear what I have to say."

"I may not want to…but I'll always listen! Thanks for your time and effort… Give my regards to Alex, though he's too honest. Bye! take care of yourself, you've grown on me." Reaches out, warmly shakes his hand, and starts her exit.

"Bye! Hildy!"

Next morning, the Sun is shining magnificently. Such a beautiful day that Nate is happy to be sharing with the rest of the World… And is overjoyed with his discovery of the latest edition of *last week's* New York Sunday Times, Theater section found at the bottom of his very own, he thinks, Waste Basket and at the moment totally absorbed in his reading of it checking on all the Broadway shows he's missing and reading the reviews on 2 new openings. Nate quietly sipping his coffee on *his* 'Park Bench'… When the Mayor jogs onto the Scene, halts in front of him. Nate looks up to what at first appears to be an apparition. But *Hell No!* it's The Mayor… *" Mornin' Mayor!"*

"Mornin' Nate!"

"Like Cyrano De Bergerac you might at least have called me Nate the Enigma, Nate the Eccentric, or…Nate…does he not remind you of Nietzsche for his views of a Master race? That's what you might have said… But not to worry! I've been called many things in my lifetime!"

"I prefer Nate the Man, Nate the Friendly, Nate the Kind…Or simply Nate… But this is not a social call. I've come to warn you that because you have once again come to the Public's attention with your Radical Views, this according to my overpaid industrious, Investigative Staff … *That* there are some out there who claim you're a threat to their peace of mind. And that these same *Types* might want to do you in! Say… Lop your head off as they do in some places of the world. Some of whom that didn't like that you won a Pulitzer or your political views while in that D.C. Think Tank, or thought you crazy when you predicted 911."

"Nonsense!" "Nate responds in disbelief, "I'm just this old Bum minding my own business Mayor, you know that !"

"I may know you're innocent of their worst fears but now that *you're* seen as clandestinely rising like a huge Phoenix from the ashes! Brand you as a troublemaker! ... An Oracle with strange and even *Supernatural* powers! That needs to be dealt with!""

"Lop my Head off?... Dealt With?... Do me in?... You gotta be kidding" *This is too much even for Nate's sense of humor as warped as it is and he breaks into convulsive laughter!*

"Wish I were –What would you say to some protection?

"From what, a rabid *rat*?"

" *Rats!* That hate an Intellectual activist like yourself, even one that retired from the world. Your ideology represents a potential danger to their cause."

"They're only opinions, with no government, army, or political clout behind them. It's still little old derelict me inside this skin. And I'm no threat!"

"I *like* your views. Why the Senator even listens to you. That's what worries those in power. They're afraid you have some magical, diabolical power and secrets that you alone are privy to. And they want you to share them with them or see you in Hell! Seems the Chinese even got word of your scheme to bring the Great Wall of China to the U.S. Border with Mexico. Now China and the Chinese here are in a funk over it!"

"Mayor put the World on notice! That I'm a destitute man in beggars clothing. Mean no harm; have no mysterious powers. Tell'em I just want to be left alone! But have a strong need to speak out!"

"I know but there are some that don't care to know it; and see you as a Big-assed threat!... I'm thinking about putting on some low profile security guys, disguised as street people, to keep you safe."

"Waste of taxpayer money!"

"What do you care?... You don't pay taxes!"

"*Don't* make money either! Unless you tax---handouts, papers, bagels and coffee, I find in the trash and gifts from society?"

"You've got me convinced. And as far as protection you don't feel any need for it then?"

"Yes!... I say--- *No* to protection!"

"Well you be sure to let me know if you should change your mind...*Ok?* ...Whoa! Almost forgot, brought you some fast food....Egg-muffin and coffee."

"Thanks Mayor for lookin' out for me."

"Take care Nate!...I lose a friend if they hurt you. Let me know if you change your mind! You hear?"

"Will do! Thanks, you're a good friend. Not to worry, I'll be fine... Bye!"

"See you!"... As he jogs off across the Park, concerned over his new friend Nate!

Nate resumes his arduous routine--- sits, reads, eats, feeds pigeons and squirrels looks up occasionally to watch passersby, checks his piece of sky, enjoys the ultra-high wind swept cloud formations and weather conditions. Being the outdoorsman he is figures the good weather to hold. Seems nowadays he's getting pretty good at foretelling impending storms and such. Satisfied with his weather forecast gets back to reading when surprise who should the wind blow in but his Buds, Harry and Mary.

Mary all excited about something. Nate never having seen her this excited about anything before, and loudly sings out his name, "Nate! Nate!... Harry here... Our very own Harry... Why he...he got ...whadya call that Har ?....A...uum?"

"A *callback*! A callback to an *Off Broadway show*...for a supporting role. They said so far I was the strongest contender and most aromatic for the part, called it type casting, didn't insult me a bit, I must say. They liked me because they correctly figured me for a method actor who--- dressed for the role, didn't shave or shower, had a real derelict look and smell to me. Then when I proved I could act; that really got'em."

Nate asks, "How'd you find out about it?"

"*Just plain luck!* Mary and I were quietly walking along counting the Pizza rinds on Mac Dougal Street, when suddenly there was this line and Mary..."

"Yeah like I boldly asks this actor in my most sophisticated voice what was goin down?... He says it was this open call for a show called "The Derelicts." I whispers to Harry the actor here, what's this open call stuff? And..."

"*Naturally* me being the method actor that I am but currently out of work inform my bud Mary... It's simply an audition where anyone can apply and do their thing for those hybrids conducting the thing, the producer, the director, you name it they're all behind this long folding table or out in the darkened theater assessing your assets, abilities, how you look, for various roles, how you sound... and damn it, if you can you act? So anyone that comes along can audition, even the real article like me, and Mary if she wanted to. And the Miracle of it all was...."

Mary jumps in, "As soon as we hit that line, it's as if the plague hit NYC. The Sidewalk cleared, the Earth opened wide. And a *Stink Hole* happened!"

"That's Sink Hole Mary, Sink Hole! Lucky for us we were in our worst, unrefined-finery!"

Mary living the role now and like a *Swell*... " True we had this small amount of body odor about us... When suddenly like a miracle we found ourselves at the head of the line!"

"No one gave us a hard time for bein' there either. They just melted away with their handkerchiefs over their noses and mouths! Right Mar?"

"It was like in duh Bible when suddenly the Nile Parted allowing the people to cross!... Well this crowd departed as far to the rear as traffic would allow, right Har?"

"Right! Noses still covered with handkerchiefs."

Nate totally absorbed and fascinated now; with a touch of *facetious,* "Amazing! Can't for the life-a-me understand why Harry?"

"Me neither... So we saunters in ...me and Mary..."

"Me in my worst dress ever; lookin'...would you believe...like a coupla Bums that come over from the Bowery...where we had a busy morning washin' windshields for tips from motorists who didn't want their windshields wiped with no dirty rags. And Harry what was that you said to me...?"

"Ah *Yes* my little chickadee!" He does his W.C. FIELDS imitation for his friends at least once a day... " Little did they know they were dealing with *West Village Swells.*"

"Yes *Dahling.*" As she goes into her best Meryl Streep impersonation... "And whose 5th Avenue address just happens to be 'The WAS'...Which we had to explain was Washington Arch Square. Named by this *Dahling* friend of ours Nate Nicols, a Pulitzer Prize winning professor... Right *Dear*?"

"Obviously!... You could see they were immediately impressed, that we should go to such great lengths to transform ourselves into Derelicts. So they offered us a call back and said they probably could use both of us, me for an important supporting role seeing as I have the Chops and pretty good acting credits.

"And me, a walk on, with a coupla lines. Though I have little or no experience... Because they said I was the perfect female for the role visually and aromatically!... I tell you when I walked outa there I felt ... 10 feet tall!"

"You my friends," Nate proudly, grandly announces, "never cease to amaze me...Good luck at the... the call back!"

"Nate! Nate! Harry the expert says, It's a No! No! to say Good Luck! Actors say Break a Leg! I don't know why, how can you perform wit a broken leg? That's what you said Harry right?"

"Right on! But it's more like a talisman! To protect actors from bad things happening, it's *Tradition!* Whenever you do a show.... *Mairde!* Is good too spread around too!...Verbally of course."

Nate a little incredulous, "Mairde is good?"...

Harry jokingly says, *"Shit Yes!"*

"What about?"... Adds Mary, "Or, In Bocca a Lupa? You said, means in the Mouth of a Wolf... I ain't gonna stick my head in the mouth of no wolf! I don't care how lucky it is! Actors are weird, I have ta say, *Dahling!*...He also warned me if I get thu role, not ta whistle in the dressing room. But if I do..."

Harry asserts, "Walk around in a circle 3 times Mar and spit!"

"You see what I mean Nate...Actors are Weird!"

"Thank God for that! Where would we be without'em, Har?

"Damned right!"

"Listen to this bit of news everyone!" Nate brags, "the Mayor jogged into my life a short time ago to tell me there are... are you ready for this? People that would want to do me harm!"

"*Heeey!...* You're kidding right? " Harry asks. ... I mean like what did you ever do to them?"

"Nothing!... I seem to be a threat to them with my infamous background!"

Mary with deep feelings for Nate can't believe her ears. "They gotta be Loonies! Right? You are the sweetest man I know...in fact actually, you and Harry are the two sweetest men, I've *ever* known."

"Nat doffs his stained Yankee baseball cap to her, says thanks."

Harry does a little bow adds his, "Thank you madam!"

"Can you guys believe he actually offered me protection?"

"You got to be kidding," Harry says, "the Mayor of NYC wants to give you protection? You don't even pay taxes!"

"I mentioned that and it didn't faze him one bit."

"What'd ya tell him?" Mary asks.

"Not to bother!"

"Good for you!" Harry commands! "We have to maintain a certain *independence* and lack of fear here in the park."

"Decorum!" Nate states.

" *Privacy!*... We just want to be left alone. After all we have ow-aah dignity! Mary adds with pride.

"Right! Even though one day I may be a successful Off Broadway Actor... One thing for certain is, we don't *seek* fame. But if of course it should happen to come our way that'd be alright too!... What are you gonna do Nate?"

"Nothing!"

Harry agrees, "Perfect!"

Mary agrees, *"Nothing!*... is good!"

"Way to go!" Harry confirms all with "Always keep in mind we are here for you."

"Yes!" Mary reinforces it with, "and will be at your side if needed."

"Thanks!"

"But Alas! Seeing as at this moment you're not in need of our protection, Friend Nate...It's essential that on this gorgeous day we'll have to take leave of you, Sir Oracle and get into our roles, me as the Supreme and most Odiferous Derelict ever and Mary as a close runner-up!, right Mar?...Aah but in private life soon to be considered Swells!

Mary totally agrees! "Right you are Harry *Baby*." As they both proudly saunter off!

" See ya later! At our Salute to Sunset, followed by our Current Events meeting at my abode!"
Mary and Harry, *as they exit.* "We'll be there!"

Nate deep in thought and with some concern over his safety, which he pride fully refuses to divulge to anyone, suddenly jumps up as if to ward off a bad dream and does some jogger stretches, sits back down again and reads himself to sleep!.

Sunset

Nate, Mary, Harry, and Nan are all busily engaged in the Sunset ceremony at Nate's personal bench facing the setting Sun to the West with their very own incantation borrowed from Will Shakespeare… "But soft what light on yonder High-Rise breaks! Sleep Fair Sun! Give the frail, pale moon, its due! Though she's Cool and you much warmer too! Till tomorrow we'll make do!"… Then slowly head for his abode in

the Arch chanting, "Though she's Cool and you much warmer too! Till tomorrow we'll make do!"... When they arrive at his pad, Nate always the good Host lights candles, while overhead the work-light burns brightly. Puts on his soiled but serviceable black cape, saved for special occasions, his favorite, stained black baseball cap, backwards. *Now* dressed in his official Oracle outfit, sits in his special chair. Mary in hers, Nan sits Yoga fashion, and Harry sits on the floor, legs tucked under. They are ready!

Nate announces as is his custom, "I now call this Forum to order;" *rings the tarnished brass hand bell* 3x, as he continues, "here where opinion, controversy, worldly events, politics, are discussed freely by our Extinguished Council of Pundits... Nan please if you would start things rolling! "

Rises slowly, untwisting herself from her twisted yoga position. "You bet!...We're privileged to have with us this evening a number of Pundits from the real world: Nate Nichols former Denizen of a D.C. Think Tank. Myself, chair of the Brownstone Brown-Nosers Committee, Mary, prominent ex-addict from, 'There's Method in our Methadone U.' the Cities Drug Rehab Center.... And Finally Harry, ex-army Lieutenant, Veteran of 2 Wars, Iraq and Afghanistan, Ex-English teacher, Off-Off Broadway actor whose duties include Chair of 'The Was' Bench Committee... A word to the uninitiated who may overhear this; the Park is Home to creative people, occupying their time sleeping, schlepping, acting, reading, singing, playing Chess, collecting deposit cans and bottles, and the delightfully palatable, delectable food delicacies, preferably not too fresh but aged for maximum flavor... One side bar here, Harry is winding down his studies of Meds at Methadone U. in NYC, City of Dreams and will soon graduate with honors! Let's hear it for Harry!" Starts applause .

Everyone applauds then shouts out! "Harry! Harry! Harry!"

Harry Leaps up, proclaims! "Thank you for that splendiferous intro. But mustn't forget our mentor and friend Nate Nicols, *Relinquished Fellow* of the Bloggers Institute of Cynics, known affectionately as BIC. Whose slogan we've adopted: 'When in Doubt, ' Stick-Your-BIC!'... Under his breath "Where the Sun don't shine!"..... Let's hear a loud cheer that won't have the cops arrest us!"

All very weakly manage, "Yay-Hooray!"

Harry now grandly rising announces, " Mary of "Methadone U has something very profound to add... Mary if you please!" As he ungracefully plops down.

Mary is more the *Ham* than we were brought to realize and this performance of hers is pure tongue in cheek but doesn't let on to it right away. As she suddenly jumps out of her chair screaming. "You bet your ass---mister! I thought you were going to ignore me!... The days of ignoring women and keeping them slaving in the kitchen and with housework are over get that through your chauvinist skulls!... There I'm glad I got that off my mind!... On with the meeting for represented here tonight are: Right Wing, Left Wing, and Center!... BIC's at the ready!... Whose keepin' tha minutes here?"

Nate asks, " Nan if you will? All are called to *disorder!* All factions being duly represented... Any attempts at being politically correct will be deemed out of order!"

"Have my quill, know the drill!" Nan says, *as she holds up her Notebook to confirm it.*

"Nate would you kindly grant Handsome Harry and youthful Mary the floor for a bit of good news?"

Nate quick to respond in his official capacity, "Certainly !"

"Now hear this! I, method actor, am about to portray, a
    supporting role in the soon to open Off-Off Bway comedy,

"The Derelicts." To which you're all invited... *Mary* do you have something to add?"

"Why of course! And me , Mary am doin' tha part of Della, a former Vamp now a Camp of a Bag Lady; with a... *Sordid Past!"* Harry says it's type casting, right Har?"

"Absolutely the best type casting on God's earth!"
Everyone joins in with tumultuous *applause* and "Yay!"
"We're obviously both, type cast!"   Harry admits.
"And do I have lines or what Harry? A regular pro, I am."
"You are that Mary and just think, we get paid to Act!"
Everyone chimes in with Ad-libs of Congratulations! Some Shouting, " Break a leg!"
"Mr. Oracle if I may have your ear?
Nate declares, "The chair recognizes Mary."
"*Yes!*... Now as I get more sober and clean am beginning to feel like I gotta speak out against injustice as I believe the Sunshine club should do and become proactive in changing things for the better!"

Nate says, "Great idea Mary, glad you're beginning to realize we all need to be Proactive to change the world!"

"Thank you for that Nate!... Now these are the issues as I see'm!... We the homeless, the indigent, jobless, disabled need more, and safer Shelters; and food pantries! With job opp's for all, including Vets who went to War, lost jobs, limbs, and wound-up unemployed and destitute like many of us in the streets."

"Way to go!" Nate shouts! *While they all applaud.* "Excellent Mary! We need to take these issues and make'm our Goals! Bring'em to the attention of the authorities; and see to it they get addressed!"

All agree, " Yes! Yes!"

Nate getting silly! "I'll have my staff deliver our demands downtown to City Hall, upstate to Albany; then south to D.C. We'll demand satisfaction!"

Mary admonishes him, "can we stay serious Nate? Aren't you taking my suggestions seriously and gonna do somethin' about'em? These here issues cry out for action and need to be addressed!"

Nan says, "Listen up Nate!... Mary, those are great ideas! Let's put aside our differences, so we can work together on this!"

"*Sure!* But how and where do we start?" Mary asks.

"Well" Nan advises, "By getting involved in serious campaigning, and problem solving for starters!... Then *Networking* with people I've met who can help our cause by volunteering, donations, publicity and promoting legislation!"

"I like what's happening here!" Nate agrees. What started as joshing has turned into a campaign...I'm proud of you! Let's do it!... We'll all help! Right Harry?"

"Bet your ass!"

"Got that Nan?" Nate asks.

"Bet your ass!... got it! Now if we at least get City Hall to listen to us we'll be off to a flying start!"

"Great Nan!... Thanks Nate!... I for one am grateful. This is *real* for me!"

Nate inquires, "*Guys!* What are the hard core solid issues here?"

"Well there's Job *Outsourcing?*" Nan offers, Why are our jobs going overseas to foreigners from Ireland, India the Philippines, with the use of satellites. When we have unemployed people ready, willing, able; educated, and skilled, that can handle those jobs. It's crazy but true! Sure we're buying goods cheaper! But made *Overseas* some with slave or prison labor... I say let's declare a moratorium on it! Get back to manufacturing in America and selling our *own* goods, and pay those salaries to Americans and ease the high rate of unemployment!"

Mary adds, "What about work training programs to help teach job skills to willing workers?"

Harry suggests, "Why don't we do what Franklin Delano Roosevelt did as president during the Depression and create real jobs with organizations like the WPA, CCC and Work Camps, with all kinds of Construction Projects to rebuild bridges and parks etc. Even had a WPA branch to help jobless theater people and by putting thousands of others to work."

All go a little nuts with Cheers and Applause!#~!*+*~!~~!*

"Bravo everyone!" Salutes Nate, "for that list of Issues that need fixing!... You've obviously done your homework!... And there might just be some things we can do to stem the tide of imports... *On the lighter side.* Consider your own garments, shoes, you'll see almost nothing is made here anymore." *As he Mockingly checks his raggy clothes.* "With cheap foreign overseas labor to undercut U.S. prices we can't compete! Except by enforcing controls with embargoes, tariffs, and trade agreements, then and only then we might stand a chance... You can see the dilemma we're in?" They all manage a *nod.* "So then when I'm made President of the League of Decadence; which deals with the Rise and Fall of the U.S., these issues will be addressed and corrected to put this country in a survival mode...We don't want to wind up like Rome, a hundred of years ago crumbling to ruins through decadence and into Doom!"

They all chime in with, *Ad libs.* " Boo!... Boo!... Get Serious!... Stop clowning Nate!"

"I am serious! Alright then, 'Our Platform' will be built on providing jobs for Americans, by eliminating outsourcing! It's a simple solution; offer jobs to Americans first and with a *Living Wage*! And ideally put our jobless and Vets to work!

All, applaud, cheer, with ad libs! "Yay! Okay!... Way to go!"

Harry rises suddenly, jerkily to his feet, starts pacing like a wild man then dramatically but honestly speaks. "Listen to this Tale of Horror!... Awhile back a couple of rusty ships anchored off Queens, their passengers, *hundreds of Chinese,* as Indentured Servants who paid for their journey to the States, some paying with their lives. All for the sake of freedom, and many of whom had to swim ashore to begin life in the U.S. with these words carved in their minds, "Give me Your Tired your Poor." Etc.... Indenture, isn't that Slavery?... Didn't Lincoln put an end to that with the Emancipation Proclamation?"

"Wow Harry! I heard about that on the news." Nan answers, that's Powerful, and Relevant! As Armageddon itself!"

"Let's bring and insist on a Plan of Action," Nate commands, "on the best way to bring these issues to the attention of our leaders!"

"May I have the floor?" requests Harry!

"The chair recognizes Harry"...

He rises slowly, deliberately and cuts loose with a powerful summation... " **All these issues are our 'OUR Epiphany Nate!'** I sense a powerful *Vibe,* since, like Nate who served in Vietnam. I've seen War up close and personal in Iraq and Afghanistan! And now... *Vow* a War on Poverty ! As a Citizen to *Promote Peace!* Shouting it out to the Politicians, Diplomats, Jingoists and Profiteers that we're sick and tired of WAR! 'And we're not gonna put up with it anymore! *Damn it!'*

All now ***Vigorously applauding and shouting it out! "This is Our Epiphany!... Our Epiphany!***

"You've struck the mother lode Harry!" Nate announces, "A peaceful assault on the hierarchy to bring this Blood-Bath, this money lust for War to a Halt!"

Nan boldly proclaims, *"This* is our July 4th! Our Bastille Day! We'll Rise Up! We'll *Protest!* Peacefully, with Boots on the Ground!"

"Right on Nan! A cause Celebre! From a determined handful of citizens!"

Mary in her most shrilly, assertive tone , "True! We'll start a Tsunami! Bombard our leaders with Words, Actions, Deeds! Unlike the B.S. they feed us!... Hit the streets! 'We the Street People, the Homeless, the Indigent, the Jobless, and Vets ' of New York shall rise up and march for what *We* believe in, *Our* side of the story, and picket; carrying signs made from cardboard boxes; that we 'The People of the Street' live in!"

"Now hear this World! Nan Goodhart being the Computer Nerd that I am will now employ the latest in Social Networking Media which is Worldwide to bring on these *Changes!* And get volunteers and funds from around this crazy but generous world of ours!"

"Guys, *terrific!"* Nate Shouts-Out! "I've never seen you fired up like this. You inspire us all; *now* it's time to inspire **The World!** Convert ourselves to become *Activists,* not *satirists,* sitting on our hands like the babbling, infighting Politicians who can't seem to pass any decent legislation these days! Who are too busy getting re-elected and pandering to the lobbyists! Let's bring an end to this thirst for WAR, the hunger, and provide good jobs and a living wage, and affordable housing for those in need and handicapped!... Time to take to the streets, March--- Protest! And use Social Networking! This is great thinking Nan , Mary and Harry! To all of us here I say Yay Hooray! Let's get started today!... It's Time for *Our Plan of Action!"*

Everyone cuts loose with ***Excited Cheers and Ad libs!***

Nan now strongly demands , " No more Talk! Let's show the world what a Minority with a cause can do! And get the **Underprivileged Majority,** to take a stand and have the Media and Social Networks take notice and send out our message to the World!

"Yes!...Yes!" Shouts Mary! "See what you started Harry?

"Way to go *Mary!... You* threw the Hail Mary Pass!"

Nan anxious to get started, "Nate, what's the plan?"

"Your Oracle is Thinking! Thinking!... I'll have it... in a New York Minute, it's *Brewing! ...Brewing!...Wait!...* But *First...* let me digress on *Why* Politicians declare WAR, then have Libraries built as Monuments to their legacy, (in an *aside) to feed their thirsty Egos!*... Is it that they simply crave *Sainthood* in the eyes of the Public! While it would appear they rarely support Peaceful Solutions!... Now then, *Back!* to OUR PLAN, gotta be a Super Active One!...We'll start by meeting here tomorrow at 8 A.M.! Ready to March and Chant our Hearts out for Our Cause!"

"YES! YES!" they all shout in unison! *Then burst into one humongous cheer!*

Harry proud of his Oracle, "Nate you're a man of action!"

Nate takes command now, "Anyone with connections uptown, raise your hand!... *Nan try to recruit them and sell them on our cause!...* Good! that's a start. Remember! tomorrow morning at EIGHT! We'll March up Fifth Ave. to the *Library* at 42 St. then East, brandishing our signs; right to the UN and Picket! Yes Picket! Aren't we forgetting something here? ...*Signs!*... We need *Signs!"*

"Piece –a-cake!" Says Mary, "I'm an activist-artist... Let's not forget we gotta make a point of the Homeless and Vets, sleeping in boxes, by using cardboard for signs. The public needs to see and feel that kinda image with these here signs!"

"Mary, *Alleluia!" Practically sings it,* "You're the one that should have the PhD, you're right on the money with that! Soo...?

"I can help you with that Mary." Nan says, "I'm not bad myself."

"What a team we'll make--- 'The Derelict and the Aristocrat!" You're on! I been a protester since I was a kid, and can handle felt markers wit the best of'em!"

"Mary meet me at my palatial Brownstone at 6:00 A.M... You know--- the one with the Lions out front!... And don't worry about boxes; felt markers and string, I have plenty! I'm a regular pack rat!... Then we'll meet the men here!"

"You bet! If you could put on some coffee, I'll be happy as a squirrel at a nut farm!"

"Sure! I'll even throw in an English Muffin, I'm partial to'em! And some nuts."

"Terrific, I'm beginning to like *Protesting* thing!"

"8 A.M. tomorrow!" Nate bellows, "and we'll do our best for the U.S., the Homeless, Jobless and Vets, the Indigent, Disabled you name it!   I now declare us full blown activists!... Any objections? --- None? Ok then ! Nate the Oracle of Was now declares this meeting officially over!... Nan mark that in your Logbook Register!" *She merely nods; this gal is efficient!. Then rings his official Bell*... "Night all! See you bright and early tomorrow!"

All jubilantly shout out! "Goodnight Sir Oracle!" *He unwinds, it's been a tough day...as they noisily, happily, excitedly exit.*

Chapter Six

The Pickets

*N*ext morning. The Sun barely, timidly appears. Winking through an early morning smog at Nate and Harry's meeting place The Park Bench, near the WAS!

Harry edgy because the women haven't showed up, wonders out loud… "Where's the Hell's Mary and Nan? We gotta get going! Our public awaits us…Besides the longer we picket the better our chance of being noticed by the Media and our cause brought before the public."

"Right! But relax Harry! They'll be here shortly. Probably got delayed making *Signs*."

Minutes later they hear, chirp! chirp! Not the chirping of birds but of 2 women all excited! … Could it be?…Well what the Hell?

… Nate realizes it's none other than Nan and Mary, one out talking the other, if that's possible?… Both men now happily relieved! "It's them! Nate shouts out! Jumps up and warmly welcomes them, "Mornin' ladies we were about to send out an APB on you two lovelies!..."

Nan & Mary, carrying and wearing signs; appearing like a dazzling, ghostly apparition. "Good Morning troops! Sorry we're late." Says Nan apologetically.

"I take full blame!" Says Mary, "It was my idea to get the biggest *Bang,* for our buck. So I sez to Nan let's print the signs like *front*, and *back* Billboards; covering our Goals for the Homeless, Jobless, Disabled, Addicted and Vets. Telling the World we have 2 Vets marching with us to make our point!"

"Way to go everybody we're on the right track!" Nate encourages his troops.

"Mary and I were very happy with our Billboards which we printed in bold letters. Then I figured, why not *flyers*? So I printed up a bunch that we can hand out!"

"This way the people can take our message home with them and tell their family and friends." Mary adds proudly.

"Fantastic ladies!" Nate declares, "This gets better all the time!"

"What- a-Team! What-a-Team!" Harry loudly affirms!
From Nate, "Let's have a look!"

Nan and Mary proudly pass them copies.

By now they're all laughing and kibitzing as they put on their *Billboards*, like kids at a picnic! *Comments* flying!..."*Hey this is great!*"..."*Yay we're Official activists now!*"... "*Way to go!*"--- *While they help one another putting on the signs.*

Mary outa control now! "Wow this is exciting! … Official Activists! … We'll show'em! March straight up $5^{th\ Avenue}$ we will!"

Nan top of her voice now! "Hey Everybody repeat *this*

MANTRA! As we Hit the streets all the way up FIFTH AVE. Let's GO! And Sing out! ***'Peace! Peace! Let All War Cease! May Jobs, Food, Shelter for all Homeless and Vets, Disabled, and Addicted Increase!'*** ...Over and over! Till our gums hurt, and our feet smart!"

Nate asserts, "What- a- team!" As they start hoofing it up *Fifth* singing out their beloved Mantra as they Go!

"Peace! Peace! Let All War Cease!' May Jobs, Food, Shelter for all Homeless and Vets, Disabled and Addicted Increase!"

Later, *tongue's blistered , vocal chords sore, voices raw, feet getting blistered, billboards twisted, feeling heavy. They bravely, jubilantly arrive at their destination in front of the UN. When Nate boldly takes charge.*

"Sing out Troops but ***alternate*** our mantras, for all the World to hear! So we don't ***Bore but Soar!"***

All now reviving-cranking up their enthusiasm, Picketing and repeating their famous Mantra, playing to the uncaring, unconcerned, disinterested traffic, motorists, passersby; against a cacophony of traffic noise.

"Peace! Peace! Let All War Cease!"

Then on impulse they All stop! Face out, as Mary speaks out!

"Down with War! It's pandemonium! Let freedom ring! Stop All the Damned-War-ring!"

Then they *All* resume picketing and chanting their Mantra.

"Peace! Peace! Let All War Cease! May Jobs, Food, Shelter for all Homeless and Vets, Disabled, and Addicted Increase!"

Now the *Hecklers* have their day yelling out over our

determined Activists' Mantra trying to drown them out!
Heckler: "Hey ain't I seen youse sleepin' in the gutter?"
Harry the Actor to Heckler, " Yeah! Next to your *Brudder!"*
As they don't miss a beat continuing their Mantra……. **"Peace! Peace! Let All War Cease!"**

They All Stop! Face out!

Mary takes stage, loudly to the small number of gatherers.

"We're irate, War is not our fate! End All War before it's too late!

Motorist: *"Hey!...* Where'd you get dem clothes from, *Sucks*

5th Avenue! Ah---ahahahaha……..!

Mary the demure bounces back with, "Nah! From your wife's closet! Bozo!
" Zapped him good Mar!" Compliments Nate.
Nan coming out of her shell gives a yell! "Bombs kill & maim! Bring home our GI's whole not lame!"

A Motorist, "Hey Bimbo! You belong in Limbo?"

Nan shouts out! " And live near you **Jocko**!"

All, *Chanting.* **"Peace! Peace! Let All War Cease! May Jobs, Food, Shelter for all Homeless and Vets, Disabled, and Addicted Increase!'**

Then suddenly, deliberately Stop for effect!
Motorist: "Give it a rest! You're distoibing my thinking!"

98

Nate loudly joins in, "And promise not to distoib your *Drinking!*"

Motorist: "Hey crud you're giving the sidewalk a bad name!"

Nan getting wound up, " Dirtbag that was Lame!"

Once again they resume picketing and mantra. **"Peace! Peace! Let All War Cease!"**

Nate suddenly halts his troops with, "Hold your Mantras and picketing for a *MO!*.... Let's talk!... Am I hallucinating but am I not seeing hide nor hair of *the Media converging on us?*

Mary insists, "Give it time! Give it Time! Watch! The Media will explode onto the scene with Copters, reporters, cameras, and recorders promoting our cause! Flashes blinding us! What a moment! We'll be on the cover of Time and Rolling Stone!

"Networks will be fighting over us!" Harry adds, "They just haven't spotted us!"

Nan encourages them with, "Any minute now we'll be Blitzed by the Media!"

"This is your Leader speaking and I say into the Breach, The Battle is not yet Won! *Troops!*...Sing out those Mantras loud so All the World Will Hear!"

They All get back to their Chanting and picketing. **"Peace! Peace! Let All War Cease!"**

Motorist: "Hey Skid! Where'd ya get dem clothes from the Salvation army!"

Mary not to be outdone counters with, "Outa your closet, Sid!"

Wise-ass Bystander: "Give us a break! Take a shower take a bath you're making the air smell *Real* bad!

Harry blasts her with, "That's your *breath* Lady!"

Now who should drive-by but John Law blaring on his Bull Horn rudely announcing in his worst New Yorkeese. "Get off-a thu street before we call the paddy wagon and chrow youse all in jail! Maybe that'll cool your heels and mouths!... Ya Wanna protest, get a permit! Ain't nobody been granted no permit here!... Break it up now! Or we'll chrow youse all in thu Wagon! Wit pretty shiny bracelets on your ankles an' wrists!"

Nate in a shout out! "What about our First-Amendment Rights, you ever hear of that officer?"

This Cop doesn't drop a stitch with perfect gramma' says, "Not without no permit! So get your butts outa here! Or Else!... Got it? "

Mary practically screaming she's so upset! "Officer we have a perfect right! But you can't do…………"

The good officer of the law cuts her to the quick with, "Bet your butt we can!... Better get movin' lady! And all of youse before I *read* you your rights!"

"Come on gang let's leave peacefully!" Nate orders, before they cuff us; like in a totalitarian state! We'll *Regroup* at 'The WAS' and to *All* concerned *We Will Be Back!*... And with a permit?... We're going officer; we don't blame you, you're just doing your job!"

"That's so kind of youse Mister! Now beat it! Before I cuff youse all! And give you an all-expense- paid tour of Police Headquarters!"

Discouraged but inwardly vowing to be back again leave mumbling under their breaths, what they're mumbling they don't dare let the officers of the Law hear or it would be *Coitins* Sweetheart!

The Nightmare!

That night in Nate's abode, he starts to read, then getting a lot agitated with the lack of results on their first picketing adventure and the indignity of it all with those rude cops insisting they had no right to be there... *"Who says?"* he asks out loud. Turns to a classical station on his scratchy transistor radio... Hears sounds of someone entering down below, *"That you Nan?* But there's no answer... *Mayor!* You doing a little late night calling?...Mary?...Harry?....Who's there? Gets up quickly to investigate, checks the stairwell... Thunder is heard in the distance! Nate does not return..............

Ⴐhe park *next morning is bathe in bright Sunshine with The Sunshine Club assembled and all set to Welcome it!... Except Nate!...* **NO NATE!**

Nan's curiosity is killing her, she' beginning to worry asks, "Anybody seen Nate?"

"Ain't seen'm," Mary nervously answers, " I'm beginning to feel like this is very unusual for Him not to be here."

" Likewise" Harry worried says, "Let's go! It's no fun welcoming the Sun without the Sunrise Club's founding father, and Mentor."

"Our very own Oracle!" Mary nervously utters.

Nan playfully, "Our friend and sleep in!"

"Now *I'm worried,* Harry says, "with all that talk of somebody wanting to do him in! We'd better check! He *never* sleeps in."

"You bet! And have a look! Mary shakily mutters, " Now I'm *scared!"*

*They quickly walk to the Arch, enter it, impatiently,
breathlessly climb the spiral staircase ... Minutes later... As
they're entering Nate's abode we hear them calling out!...* "Nate
you Ok?... Nate sleepin' in?... Nate?" "Nate?" Beginning to build
in pitch when they get no response to their calls for him! "Nate
answer!" ... "Nate?"......................................???
But *No* response... *Nooo* response! As they look frantically
around for signs---and finding **nothing! Nothiiiinnng!**.......

"There's nothing to go by" Nan notes, "I don't see any signs of
a struggle! The place in its usual disarray who can tell anyway?"

"His maid must have the day off! Jokes Har, "Kidding aside
there's no pools of blood or body parts around."

"Would you stop that Harry" Mary chastises him, "We need a
plan of action! Nan would you ...?"

"Of course!... I'll go to my house immediately and call the
Police."

Harry reminds her, "Better call the Mayor! Nan!"

Mary says, "And Senator Hildy!"

"Not to worry, I'll try'em all!"

"Leave no headstone unturned!" Naturally Harry. has to get a
comment in!"

Mary really annoyed now, "Harry will you stop! **Stop!**"

*Nan unloading on him! "Harry cut the bad jokes at a time like
this or any other time!... OK! OK!... I'm off! But will hustle back as
soon as I find out something."*

"Harry whad-a-ya say we check the neighborhood! *Like*---we
could ask around?"

Harry responds, "Cool idea Mary! Let's do it!" They takeoff
together.

After the Search

THEY ALL PLANNED to *meet toward dark at Nate's abode.*
Nan is already on the scene looking for any signs of Nate's having
been there or signs of what may have occurred there if anything.
Having had no luck finding any clues. After a short time, hears
noises, of someone coming into the Arch.

Nan on the alert, "Mary, Harry, is that you?"

"Yeah it's us!" Mary answers. They quickly climb the stairs
and breathlessly enter the Abode. Hi Nan! Am I glad to see you!
Find out anything?... The cops combing the neighborhood?"

"Yeah!... Any leads?"...Harry asks.

Nan quickly responding, getting seriously emotional now,
"Cops are not interested in a missing person, until they've been
missing 72 hours. And when I mentioned he was a vagrant, the
cop *laughed!*... That's when I blew my stack and said a person is a
person, vagrant or not. Then the laughing Hyena of a cop said;
you should call the Missing Vagrant's Bureau at 1-800-Vag-rant,
they'll get right on it. Then this upstanding officer sitting on their
fat ass at the Police Station started laughing, grandstanding,
hysterically, I could hear laughter in the background. Really
enjoying this...at Nate's expense. May that cop's next arrest
have serious body odor and bad breath and throw up on them!

Harry cajoling, "Wow I can see you have a Dark Side! You
should've asked for a *female* cop... probably have more heart.

"It **was** a *female* cop!" She answers.
"Ouch!"

Mar asks, "Did you try the Mayor's office?"

"Sure!... He's attending a conference in Las Vegas."

"In Las Vegas?" Harry quizzically asks, "That's gotta be tough duty!"

"That's where a lot of conferences are held." Nan responds, "Damned if Hildy's not attending the same one."

"What about their assistants, wouldn't they help?" Mary Quizzes!"

"No! Besides they have no clout and the Mayor and Senator left word not to disturb them; unless it's a National Emergency."

Harry charges, "Nate is a National Emergency, if terrorists have him!"

"I tried that slant," Nan says, "and they just laughed. They're not interested in vagrants with Pulitzers abducted by terrorists."

"Hildy is gonna be angrier than hell over this!" Harry prophesizes.

"And the Mayor!" Injects Mary.

"You're not kidding." Says Nan, "especially when they find Nate's headless body lying on the steps of City Hall... A martyr to Our Causes!"

"What Causes?" Harry puts in his 2 cents... "Pan Handling, vagrancy, freedom to be... a Bum and *Protest?* Let me know when to stop?"

Mary now getting upset because of their kibitzing. "Stop it both of you and now!"

"*Ok!* Ok! Mar." Harry agrees, "But where do we go from here..........?"

Nan and Mary Together... "what's that racquet out there?"

Apparently unknown to our Trio, word leaked out about Nate The Oracle of Was having gone missing because of some terrorist plot, it was speculated... With some early evidence of a Media presence and a noisy crowd now gathering outside the

Arch in Washington Square Park, '*The Was!*'... *Then Suddenly there's the sound of someone entering down below.*

When they hear the friendly voice of Mayor Ed Coach crying out! "Is anybody there? It's the Mayor, with a surprise!"

"Welcome back Mayor, come on up!" Nan offers, " it's just Nate's Sunshine gang on overtime!"

They arrive a few minutes later breathless and excited!

"I brought a friend," he announces as *they enter Nate's abode,* "Senator Hildy." He adds, "HI! I heard you tried to reach me while I was at the conference. Sorry, I left word not to be disturbed, because it was a Top Secret Conference, all about Homeland Security."

"I'm sorry too, or we might have had Nate back by now. Hildy boasts. But we're here now, and we'll do our best to get him back, safely!... Any word yet?"

"Nothing Senator!" Mary sadly relates, "An' we're all seriously worried!" Mary bursts into tears ... Hildy does her best to console her, to no avail."

The Mayor joins in trying to soothe her, " Don't worry Mary we're doing our best. In retrospect he should've accepted my offer of protection."

"Hildy agrees, "And how!... The good news is, we've got *all* our agencies working on it!"

As the Street noise builds outside, the Mayor announces,

"Hear that, those are your neighbors, curiosity seekers, wanting to get the facts... Hoping to find out if his headless torso has shown up yet."

"Mayor," Harry says, "I just got yelled at for saying the same thing!"

Mary fuming, "Would you two stop talking like that!"

106

"Mary's right!" Hildy says, "Let's keep our heads!... The Media love's intrigue. And they're well represented out there. Waiting anxiously near the Arch for word about Nate's fate... Nate The Psychic! The Oracle! The Prophet who foretold 911! And nobody listened!"

Nan adds lovingly, "Our friend!"

Mary a tad ballistic, "Stop! You're making it sound like a eulogy!"

"*My,* we're getting touchy."

"Sorry Nan! I know you mean well, but I got a right to be touchy!"

The Mayor nervously says, "Listen to that crowd chant! I had the police cordon off and secure the area before they go wild, now they're even beginning to say that Nate is attracting terrorists into the City, to prevent him from forecasting *Terrorist Attacks!*

Hildy piles it on, "You should see the streets all blocked off with people shoving against the barricades. They all want to meet * the Oracle of WAS, the *MAN* who predicted 911!"

The Mayor describes the scene outside, " It's like a shrine, out there with everyone wanting to see his abode, and feel his presence. Some putting Teddies, and flowers around, even candles!"

"Treating him just like a a member of the human race that cares and foresees events before they happen!" The Senator intones, "and with the Psychic powers of an Oracle!"

"After this is over, I'm going to write a play." Harry now bragging with the Big Ego of a potential Off Broadway Super Star, and possible winner of an Obie award for best Actor at some future date.... "Call it the '*Miracle of Was.*"

"Great title Harry!" Mary cries out through her tears.

Hildy attempts to comfort her. "It'll be Ok Mary, we'll find him alive and well!"

"Thanks Mary! What are you crying about?"

107

You Harry always makin jokes about Nate and him still not found, alive or dead with his beautiful, scraggily head severed from his body from some terrible terrorist cutting it off with a huge sword" She really balls now and cries out in anguish, "see what you've done now!"

Harry all apologetic now tries to calm her. "Sorry Mary it's my nature to lighten peoples burden, the weight of sorrow is too overwhelming. That's all I intended to do lighten your load. "I didn't want to make it worse for you but ease the pain."

Mary, through her tears, "I'll be alright Har, it's just that I love this man so much, an' don't want nuthin to happen to him."

"Let's get back to reality folks, shall we!" Nan suggests, "As in, what do we do to get our friend Nate back, Mayor?... Senator?"

"Mayor profoundly says, "I feel we should wait it out! The perpetrators are bound to show their hand!"

Hildy says, "My feeling exactly; waiting's the answer everyone!... Meanwhile... maybe we'll *come up* with something."

Mary hot now, "Is that the best you Guys can do!?... *Wait?... Wait!*...for Heaven's sake? I believe in *Action!*"

The Mayor lot calmly suggests, "Perhaps they'll put a price on his head! Then we'll have something tangible to deal with!"

"You mean Ransom?" ...Nan hot now, "You've gotta be kidding! Who'd be idiot enough to attempt to collect ransom for Nate?"

Mary, almost hysterical, " I'm surprised you asking a question like that, and you say you care... *bah!* He's worth a lot! To a lot of people, just look at that crowd out there!...But more to *me*, than to you! You only claim to love him. What do know about love? All you care about is Money and what'll buy! That's you...You love his brain that's all ... *I love all of him!*"

"I'm sure you do... Yes I love his brain, his soul... And *Hate* to think what your favorite parts are?"

"Way ta go *Nan*!... Now your mind's in the gutter with mine!"

Things are really getting *Hot* between these two! *As they face off like Sumo wrestlers!*

* "Sewer is more like it!" Nan bellows, "with the rest of the feces! By the way I hear you've been voted Ms. Virus of the West Village and have gone Viral!... You, you street urchin, vagrant, ex-addict, you, you lowlife, did I leave anything out?"   She doesn't quite know what to call this, this creature she considers so a far beneath her. "Or shouldn't I ask, the medical books are full of case histories with photos and cures!'"

"*You*! You're callin'me a Feces? Dat's like the pot calling the kettle Brown... err... Black! As my sainted mother used to say when she was sober. An' I ain't got no viruses!... Now you done it! ... I'm gonna... I'm gonna, *(Trying to make up her mind what kind of hurt she's gonna put on this snob!) then lunges!*

" Ladies! Ladies!" Harry blares out as he steps between them blocking a punch from Mary. "Ouch you got some punch there lady! I wish someone cared for me as much as you two, care for him... Now calm down...CALM DOWN! *And* let's find Nate!"

"Yes! *Yes!*... Peace ladies please!" Shouts the Mayor as *he* begins to lose it now. Give it a rest, and let's search for him everywhere! Every..."

"Yes Everywhere Mayor!" Hildy interrupts, " But let's get going now before he winds up losing body parts, and we lose our man Nate ."

"Now *You* too Hildy!" Mary screeches! You had to say that, that! *Lose Body Parts thing!*... Poor Nate! Oh My poor Nate"

"Sorry Mary I didn't mean to upset you."

Mary, crying now! And voiceless can only nod.

109

While the Mayor raps up the meeting with. "**we**'ll report back with any news. Nan we'll use you as liaison, and I'll call you at home if we find out anything new."

Nan still shaken, " Yes please, I'll get the word out...And hope as we all do for it to be *Good News!* Mayor and Senator please, some--Good News! And *Thanks!*"

Harry and Mary, still rattled, manage a Big, "Thank You!"   As they all leave to go into action!

Chapter Seven

Nate's Epiphany

Sunrise 2 days after his abduction, *all members of the Sunrise Club are in Nate's abode where they've been for the last few hours.*

Mary trying to be upbeat, "What d'ya say we welcome the Sunrise today; and try to keep up the tradition in honor of our buddy, Nate?"

Nan depressed over it answers, "Nah, I don't feel up to it *without* Nate."

Me neither, Harry says, " I'm too worried …I'll wait till we get him back safe!"

"As for me," Mary says, "I'm antsy and afraid. *Like* it's going on two full days and *nuthin!* My heart wouldn't be in it!"

"I went home to check my answering machine," Nan complains, nothing there either from the Mayor, Senator, *or* the law."

"We shoulda heard somethin by now." Mary moans."

"Today's the day!" Harry proclaims, " I feel it in my bones… I saw what might've been an omen! While everyone was sleeping I thought I saw a *Spook* floatin' around, in the corner!"

"You're kidding right?" Nan in disbelief, "I mean Nate can pull that stuff off but now *you*. Was it Alexander Hamilton or John Barrymore… or George Washington, she quips ?"

"Not Barrymore, Harry explains, "this spook was sober!…. Carried himself like an officer… wore some kinda uniform."

"Sounds like Alex is trying to tell us something." Nan speculates, "You ask him anything?"

"I didn't want to wake Mary who was sleeping nearby here in Nate's little Abode. So I crept quietly over to Alex… "and whispered where's Nate? He pointed with his thumb, like maybe uptown on the Eastside. This is a wild guess on my part…………

Maybe--- Park Ave? In one of those Embassies?"

"**S**uddenly *you're* a Psychic!… Nan says, "**w**hich embassy? Where?"

"How should I know? It's just me, Harry taking a wild guess. I'm not sure of this ghost business. Could'a been a dream, or exhaust from the 5th Ave. bus. But I did confront an apparition!

112

It was *Bizarre!*... I still think we're no better off than before, unless Alex could lead us to where Nate is held?"

"I wish you wouldn't lead us--- on," Mary begs, " when it comes to Nate. It's not fair to Nan or me... Cause we're really worried here and we shoulda heard something by now."

"I'm not leading you on," Harry really concerned now, "I'm as confused and worried as you are!"

The Mayor manages to schlep in without making a sound, "Hel---uum...Hello Troops," still trying to catch his breath after that winding stairway. " Don't bother saluting it's just me, your Mayor arriving in my stealthiest fashion! But no Media! With this word I hope will help slightly... That the cops have looked under every bridge, in every cardboard box, doorway, shelter, and subway!... And zero! No reports of a headless male corpse found anywhere!"

"You hada say that Mayor, didn't you?" Wails Mary sick and tired of the sick references to her friend. "I wish everyone would stop talkin headless this and headless that; it's mindless!" She's off and crying again!

"Sorry! Didn't mean to be insensitive; just give the facts!"

" It's Ok Mayor. I meant no disrespect... I'm just worried--- *like*--- I really care for this guy!"

"We're all worried, Mary, the Senator too, though she couldn't make it, sends her best and says she's praying for him.... Wow! You should see the mob scene around the Arch, waiting for Nate's return.... And the Media! I coulda used an escort just to get me through!"

There's a loud raucous commotion downstairs just outside the Arch as we begin to hear something sounding like a familiar voice with an extreme New Yorkeese accent... See if you can recognize this voice? "Heeyeh! Like I'm the pizza delivery dude from Ciccio's Pizza. Which wit dew respect Officers ... I gotta deliver before the Pizza gets cold and the soda gets warm!... Thanks-you-

Sirs! Sings on the way up the stairs… When-a-da moon-a- hitsa yew eye like a big-a-peeza pie-dats amor-ray--- da-a-da-da-da, youra –in-a luv, da da da La La La……………….. keeps singing as he enters the landing of Nate's abode… Then makes his grand entrance wearing a baseball cap turned sideways, and sunglasses. "Hey! I got yore Pizza like youse ordered. That's twenty bucks! If you please! Wit da tax, an delivery! And of course youse can always chrow in a tip for dis overworked delivery guy! If you please."

Harry defensively, "We didn't order any pizza…did you Mayor?

"Hell no!"

"Ladies did you?" Harry asks.

Nan & Mary simultaneously erupt!… As they both recognize who it really is which blows their minds and are they crazy ecstatic, or what?"

"Nate! Nate!" From both of them, then

"You crazy, crude Dude!"…from Mary…

Followed by, "It's Nate! Nate! Everybody!" Both shouting out!

"You can't fool us!" Both scream! Over this Miraculous sighting of the Prodigal Son returning. As the full impact hits them … Suddenly they grab each other and bust out in a wild and crazy Dance!… Run over to him, crush him in a loving bone crushing Bear Hug, lifting him off the ground as they do so. Then both administer The Coup de Grace by *smothering* him with affection… Kissing the skin off his weathered face at the same time!

"Ooh Nate!" Mary shrieks!

Then Nan, " You can fool some of the people some of the time but you can't fool these 2 Broads *any* old time!"

They both attack a second time hugging and kissing him with ecstasy!

Still the Pizza-boy Nate, "What are youse doin?…Don't ya recognize a delivery guy when youse see one?"
Harry still in total disbelief! "Is that really you in there?... *Nate* you found your true calling---A singing Pizza delivery Boy!... Look everybody he *Didn't Lose* his head after all. I could swear your headless ghost would come back to haunt Washington Square!"

Hugs him; joined by the Mayor. Who jests, "What a disguise!"

Mary getting in on the fun, "It's so you!"

The Mayor, now breaks into a parody of and old Vaudeville song his deceased mother taught him when she was still able to bounce him on her knee… *"Where did you get that voice oh you lucky fellow? Where did you get that voice tell me on the level?...* And that outfit? You coulda fooled me!... By the way… We glad to see *youse!"*

"I was desperate," Nate confesses, "When I saw the crowd; I figured the only thing left for me to do was to grab a pizza box and discarded soda bottle out of the garbage…to make it look real! And then to complete my ensemble put my baseball cap on sideways, *'wit sunglasses… Then! Bada-bada-bing!'* I was transformed into one Cool Delivery Dude, voice and all!"

The Mayor grills him, he's gotta know the facts, "But what the *Hell* happened to you?"

"Hold on Mayor!…"First I gotta say a great big *HELLOOO* to Our Sunshine Gang!" As he goes into his *famous crazy dance.* "Wow! am I glad to see *'All-a-youse' again!'* I missed you, and I…I… thought I'd neh-verrr… he's *tearing up, now out-a-control!* …see you again! As he holds his head in his hands sobbing!

All, *Rush to Console and Crush him… so happy to see him; well and feisty.*

Nan the clown, "We wuz crazy wit worry over youse!"…
Then back to Nan the emotional, " We did everything in our power
to find you!"

Mary giving due credit, "Yeah! Nan phoned your friends, the
Mayor, Senator, Police, the CIA, everybody!"

The Mayor adding his two-bits, "We looked under every
Bridge, searched the waters around Manhattan Island, looked in
every cardboard box and alley way … for a headless derelict
body…But the Cops found *nothing* not even a hair off your
balding head!"

Harry boasts a little too, "Mary and I canvassed the
neighborhood and came up with *Zilch! (Kidding,)* Checked the
morgue but they wouldn't let us in; said we looked like Bums!"

Now the other half of the comedy team , Mary tunes in with,

"But Zilch did Brag!--- He saw you get into a black sedan with
two well-dressed bearded dudes. Then watched as it drove off into
the night!"

Harry clarifies, "Then he went off *~! He's a little *Schitzo* you
know! Then said it was a good night for him… Begged enough
to buy some Ripple Wine which he knocked off and amazingly
minutes later claimed General George Washington himself
waived to him as he rode full gallop through the park on his White
Stallion!... Zilch being his usual slightly *Delusional* *~! Self."

Nate getting emotional now but trying to make light of it says,

"Thanks for trying, my friends! Truth be known, Zilch was
right! Not about Washington but the two well-dressed dudes and
the black sedan."

Nan tearfully, "*Really!* Did they hurt you?"

Mary even more genuinely tearful not wishing to be outdone,
" Threaten to cut your head off?"

"Or your Ding Dongs?" Har has to get in *his digs!*

"*Ding Dongs!...* Harry? . *Nooo!...* When they first arrived I
thought perhaps they needed advice. So I advised them…What else

116

could they want?... I was damned scared, but tried not to show it... Then tried to dazzle them; gave'm my spiel on *Terrorism*. They were not impressed by that either. But these Dudes were sharp, and after I ran out of Babel... They took me for a ride!"

Nan in semi-disbelief that this could happen to her Nate,

"Not a *Ride?*"

(In his best Humphrey Bogart?) "Yes *sweetheart*, so I figured it was curtains for me! Ya know kid, like the jig was up!?"

"Nate you do a lousy Bogart! But Did they hurt you?"

"Sorry *sweetheart! (Still Bogart) No,* but shoved me into their

Big Black Car!"

Now Mary interrogates him, "Can you I.D. them?"

"*Stupid* they weren't--- Sweetlips!... For *muscle* they had this huge, burly driver, like everybody else, dressed for a costume ball, with beards and sun glasses for disguises... Who tied and blindfolded me with A Zorro type mask to look like we were partying. Took me on a short drive, that to me seemed like an eternity. Apparently to their headquarters, to torture and interrogate me."

"You were supposed to try to get away! Didn't they tell you that in Grad School?" Harry enquires---sternly!

"Hell, *No!* What are you Nuts? So I goes along with the Caper. Like I was James Bond with my special watch, and atomic powered pen, that would get me out of all kinds of trouble!"

Harry plays along, "Did it work?"

"Hell *NO!* The watch needed a battery and the pen leaked on my clean white shirt!"

"*Then*--- did they torture you?" Mary persists.

"Threaten you? Harry doesn't give up easily.

Nan picks up the interrogation, "Try to re-invent or put a dent in you?"

"Why is everyone so expectant, almost wishing I'd say yes? Sure they called me a Socialist Pig, a Protester, Unclean! Me who bathes without fail at least once a month... And said their reason for warring against their lovely neighbors in the Middle East was due to the fact they cared about their neighbors and desired only to alleviate poverty by blowing up obvious capitalist symbols like cars, busses and Embassies. Not at all like the U.S. where the poor were starving in the streets, without shelter from the elements; U.S. warriors coming home, Jobless their wounds unattended. Whereas in their countries Dictators were generous to the poor and the wealthy even to the extent of Sacrificing their building of Palaces, and delaying their habit of buying expensive cars!"

Nan, *Facetiously,* "That's very generous of them!"

"Then would you believe had the audacity to call the U.S. sordid and uncaring. With a broken Justice System... Whereas crime in their countries was punished humanely. If someone stole; off comes the hand, if they murdered --- Off comes the head, if women commit adultery they are *Stoned.* Simple honest punishment which keeps the crime rate down and women virginal."

Mary tiring of the hoopla! Insisting now, "But Nate what about you?"

"Though they did threaten me, changed their tactics at the last minute. Did none of those uncivilized things. Instead offered me vintage wine, loose women, gourmet food, and seductive music; IF ? ....

Mary pressing on for the truth, "Yes? *Yes?...What?"*

"I cooperated!"

Nan now in total disbelief, "Oh no! Naturally being a man of principal and honor, you didn't give in, right?

"Wrong! But only momentarily."

Nan not comprehending, "only momentarily? Oh Nate! you poor man!"

Mary getting into her acting persona, she can be the Ham as Harry well knows... doing her best *Lauren Bacall,* "Why those Dirty Rats! Seducing you with slimy street tactics, *Big Guy!"*

"I told them I'd try to cooperate, because I *valued* my life... Then they laughed which made me extremely nervous. Especially when their Huge, Big Guy flexed his tattooed biceps at me.... I was impressed. But still careful, not sure of what they were after... Playing it cautious and cagy now... I agreed to the food, the wine, and song but not the loose women. You see I value your affection girls, and my ethics. And was saving myself."

"For me?" Nan enquires.

Mary insists, *"No! ...*For me!"

To keep the peace Nate intercedes. "For both of you!... So I promised to cooperate, which I did; before they realized it was all a sham!... Then and only then did I find it necessary to employ a new tactic to impress them with... my veracity!... And quickly sucked down the food, the wine, pretended to enjoy the music... Anticipating they might realize I was unworthy of it, or of *bloodying* the sword they kept threatened me with!... Suddenly my Coup de Resistance, as Salome exotically did her *Dance of the Seven Veils."*

Mary asks, "Salami?"

Nan quickly corrects her, "Salome! Salome!...Let him talk,

Puleese!"

And then when she was about to remove the Seventh Veil…"

"You submitted?" Harry asks.

"Hardly! Because she had outwitted her overseers and me and had *9 veils on!* So in the end, she preserved her dignity!"

Harry, Mister persistent asks. "By then were you Crocked?"

Nan now with, "But didn't succumb!?"

Nate tentatively: "Well sort of !"

Relentless, Mary digs further, "What do you mean, sort of?"

"They figured something was amiss, when they asked me difficult questions like, "We understand you have pointed the finger at money laundering Institutions in the Arab Emirates, accusing them of contributing huge sums of money to the Terrorists; Al Qaeda, the Taliban etc. Then asked me their names and wanted to know my *Secret Sources* of information. I said, the N.Y. Times, Wall Street Journal and Village Voice and New Yorker. And that I simply followed the *money trail!* Godzilla didn't like my answer for some reason, and smacked me…***Hard!***"

Nan shaken, "Oh no!"

Mary even more shaken, "Did he hurt you bad?"

"Thanks for that--- *No!* He hit me on the head!"

Mary stressing, *"Don't joke!"* ...

"Who's joking?... I told him I'm merely an informed citizen! Who reads!" Then he smacked me again **Harder!** Then Godzilla again orders me to give him my sources as he's twisting my arm from its socket! I have to admit that hurt!... I repeated the 4 Media Giants to him... That confused them!... Now they didn't know what to believe. Then their resident clown trying to catch me off guard, to see if I was privy to top secret information. Asked does the President drink too much?... Vacation to Exotic places too often or play entirely too much basketball or golf?... And worse yet does his wife insist on campaigning with him?...

Deeply private, secure info, which would give them intimate information on the White House... I informed these educated, terrorist types that I had to confer with Alex for that kind of Classified information...."

"Oh *No*?" Nan blurts out, *"Not Alex?"*

"Oh *Yes!* They said, "who is this Alex?... Is he CIA? NSA?"

"Get outa here!" Harry surprised, "You didn't tell'em about Alexander Hamilton? *(Laughs!)"*

"You got it! What's funny about that, he *is* my source!"

"Yes we know!" From Nan, *"Then* what?"

"Of course they laughed; and said 'for this you're considered a Genius of great esteem? A Professor of Sociology, a PHD, a Pulitzer Prize Winner, a former member of a D.C. Think Tank and a Psychic... And then oozing out in total *Disbelief* adds the name of one of the most famous of **Oracles** from Greek Mythology, a reincarnated, **Trophonius?** ... You are Crazy! Nuts! As you would say...These Americans are *All* crazy!... And *You especially!* Who believes he sees ghosts; and talks to them... This *Dude* is a waste of our laundered money and precious **TIME!**... For this one they won't even come up with a penny of *Ransom* Money, or *Free* our warriors from their *Detention Camps!"*

"Wow!" ... Harry flabbergasted asks, "Then what?"

"They all agreed I was a waste of terrorist funds and their efforts... With the additional problem of my **severe, unbearable body odor;** bad enough to sear their eyeballs! They said... coupled with my unkempt appearance and ragged clothing giving them the impression that I was U-N-C-L-E-A-N! **Unclean!**....Then raised their voices to a fevered pitch as they shouted, *" All Westerners are unclean!"*

"Whata nerve!" Mary insulted now, "I bathe at the shelter at least twice uh month!"

"If they only knew that many Americans shower daily, some twice a day! They'd soon change their tune… They *didn't!* And hustled me out of there, blindfolded with the mask of Zorro on ! My gut tells me their *Headquarters* was an *Embassy* on Park Ave. But I'm not sure."

From Harry the All Knowing… *"Figures!"*

Their next move was to rid themselves of me with talk of fumigating the place. I believed that to be extreme, but kept mum about it. Then wound up shoving me back into the Big Black Limo!... Drove downtown to within a few blocks of 'The Was' at 8th St. and Fifth. *Shoved* me out! Like a bag of Sawdust, mask still on, so I couldn't I.D. them, or the car. Then sped away! … And though cool on the outside; I was one big knot inside…Then, a short time later was hit with a startling revelation, that I couldn't get through the police lines at 'The Was'… Then through some remarkable quick thinking on my part, Stepped into an alley and quick as you could say Up! Up! and Away! Assumed my brand new Super Delivery Guy identity and *New Persona* like a true method actor, which at one time I considered as a career… And *Ta Da!* here I am!..."

Mary overwhelmed, "What a Horrifying, Adventure!"

"And how! … Now that I've told you about *my* exciting part in all of this; tell me how you All reacted and if you were really and truly worried?"

"Absolutely and we All, Mary, Harry and I took immediate action!" Regales Nan… "My First step being to call the police… Only to have them laugh derisively and inquire who cares about a missing Bum, lady ?... Then called the Mayor's and Senator's offices, *Nate* and guess what?"

"Yes?"

" No!" Nan counters with Both were out of town at the same convention, with orders they weren't to be disturbed unless it was a National Emergency which unfortunately you're not!"

The Mayor in Self-Defense adds, Dear Nate if Hildy and I had known we certainly would have taken immediate action! If we weren't both involved in that Top Secret Security Meeting in Vegas....You can bet your **Head and Ass** on that!"

Nate proclaims warmly through tears, "Thanks everyone for trying and working so hard...I love you all!"

All with the ad libs: "That's what friends are for!" ... "Glad you're back!" They all rush him and crush him with Love once again in a Humongous Bear hug!

" Now everyone let's call it a Day!...But what a Day ...I need sleep desperately and must say goodnight! We'll meet at Sunrise ... Thank God!... Tomorrow!"

The Mayor announces, "I'll leave some security on for awhile. Nate... We don't want to lose you again!"

"Probably won't need it but thanks, I think they've had their fill of old Nate!"

"You never know! " Admits the Mayor! "Goodnight Nate!"

Night All and Thanks to All my friends !

Chapter Eight

But Soft What light Through Yonder Smog Breaks?

Next day the Sunrise Club *greets the Sun facing East, what else? Arms raised high, including the Mayor and Senator.*

They *Salute* the Sun loudly with all their joy and energy with their favorite greeting, "Yo!... But soft what light through yonder Smog breaks? It is the *Sun! What Fun!* Arise fair *Sun* and Screw the envious *Moon*, sick and pale with Pigeon *Doo so soon!*"

Then happily sing a few Bars of, "Good Morning Sunshine!... And another New Day!"

The Mayor feeling good about everything after their salute to the Sun… "That was cleansing!"
Hildy joins in, " I've never done that before… Except on my Prom night… I loved it!"

"Once when I was down to Key West," Harry says, "They *wildly greeted Sunrise and Sunset with Martinis in their hands and in their bods as they saluted the Sun!

The Mayor tipsily adds to that. " I'll Drink to That!"

"I second the motion!... It's great to be home again, and safe with my friends! … I hope My terrorist friend Godzilla was sent back to His Desert to get his just Desserts!"

The Mayor still trying to make his point. " *See!* You should have let me give you police protection! Anyway, *sorry* I was incommunicado like that… And couldn't help you!"

The Senator adds, "Me too! I would have been after those scoundrels before you could say *al-Qaeda!"*

"Probably worked out better this way!... Now if they have any nasty terrorist plans, one whiff of me will send them packing… Never to bother this decadent American *Society* again! Perhaps if we all smelled and dressed as I do; they'd leave us alone!... Now really *Fired up!*... Friends there's something I need for you to hear! While held captive, I experienced an *Epiphany!* And came to an *explosive* decision! That we must act now and re-energize Our ' *Campaign for Peace, the Homeless, Handicapped, Jobless, Street People and Veterans!' 'Agitate till we Irritate!'* Like protestors during the Vietnam War! By pressuring Washington and the U.N. to bring about World Peace!... I say! Damn the Lobbyists, the Jingoists, it's Peace, Jobs, food and shelter for the Homeless, and the Vets...*YES!*... And Full Speed Ahead! I Say, Let's do it Gang!"

"C'mon Nate!" Harry says, "How do we do that with just the

four of us? Three homeless, *Vagrants,* two of whom are Vets, one Philanthropist and an Oracle?

"But what an Oracle!" Nan insists!

Mary, Irate again! "Hey watch who you're calling a *Vagrant,* Mr. English teacha!

"Sorry Mary!"

It's Ok! Har but you can be *snide* sometimes!

"*Attention* everyone!... Harry this should address your question! After you leave tonight and I've had my beauty rest... Then *Early* tomorrow at 7 A.M., We go into action!... With, '*Our Revised-Plan!*' What I need from all your keen minds is input on how we can increase our *Boots on the Ground* for The Cause!... That's *The Key!* ...The Lightning Bolt ingredient needed for my Epiphany! Sleep on it, I want *your* Ideas! Let's all be prompt tomorrow! This is extremely important! After the Sunrise Service, we'll all meet at 'The WAS.' Including Hildy and the Mayor, if they're available and care to join us?

"I'll be there!" Says Hildy.

"Me too!" The Mayor puts in, "May have to cut out early because I'm booked with CBS which heard about your exploits, and that *you* are this *Mysterious Oracle!* They'd like to get *my* slant on you and would like an interview... If you were to get back alive, still wearing your baseball cap with your head in tact! ... Said--- I'd let'em know!"

"Tell'em I'm alive and well; and to go to Hell! Thanks anyway Mayor! You must know by now; I'm a reclusive, enigmatic, eccentric, peace-nick, pain-in-the-ass with a Doctorate, who just happens to confer with ghosts! And wishes to be left alone with my *activist, aromatic* friends in *The WAS!*"

"You *know* that's impossible!" Hildy insists, " Now that you've become this Bigger than Life Personality, Oracle Dude whom they believe owns a crystal ball; has the persona of a Solomon, a Socrates even and is sought by World Powers... *and Terrorists!"*

"Senator, Mayor, I appreciate your friendship during the short time we've known each other--- But that's final!"

The Mayor now with his pitch, "I'll tell the News-Hounds but you know they're persistent!"

The good Senator not to be outdone. "And *Relentless!* .... But *I Promise* to do what I can."

"Thank you both; I appreciate it.... I know the *Media,* if they get onto something, it's like a feeding frenzy of Great Whites, getting the scent of blood of a smelly, self-professed Oracle. Now to all my friends here I want to say I love you Dearly and thank you for what you've done; now I need to get some ZZZ's. I'm exhausted from my abduction, the fine food, wine, and Dance of the Seven veils! Thankful I still have my head on straight and can still wear my hat. Plus all this excitement... Till tomorrow Guys!"

Mary in a motherly, protective phase, "Can I stay to see that you're Ok, and see to it nobody *steals* you again!"

"Over my dead body!" Nan announces, "Hell no, *I'll* stay!... If anyone's gonna stay!"

"No way Nanny-Poo!... Any-way he'd rather have me stay, right? I'm a hell-of-a-lot more fun!"

"*Nanny-Poo?*... That's the last straw!" Out of control once again ... *rushes Mary* and shoves her toward the exit! Beat it *Smelliferous!"*

Ready for her, shoves back. *"Smelliferous?* There ain't no such word! *Me*--- beat it? The Hell I say--- I stay! *You* go!"

"Nanny-Poo?... Oh yeah!" Screeches out, "No way am I a Nanny-Poo... I'll show you--- *Smelliferous! **No! No! No!**...*Starts toward Mary again."

Then Nate the Bold, the Brave steps between them, to keep them apart... "No one stays but me!"

Mary won't give up, "No way Jose! You mustn't, shouldn't be left alone! It ain't safe with them terrorists out there! I love ya, Nate and don't want anyone to harm you! And will die for you! If I have to!"

Nan pipes up with, "Ha! Die? You always take the easy way out Mary. *You!*... You don't know anything about love!... With oatmeal for brains from all your drugging. You can't protect Nate like I can and would!"

Mary fires back, " How dare you? You... you Rich Bitch! If *my* brain's oatmeal!... *Yours* is Dog Doo! Nate you can't trust her as far as you can throw her Brownstone... I'm stayin!"

"Out you go Ladies--- and *Now!* I love you as dear friends, and ask you to leave peacefully and not kill each other on the way out. I need my beauty sleep... Harry usher the girls out! Puleeze!"

"Sure! Come on Girls let him get his Beauty Sleep! He'll be Ok! *Right?"*

"Right as rain!"

Nan can't give in not now. "But!.......""

Neither can Nate, " Outa here !"

Mary still at it, "**N**ate can't I?"

"Out!... Harry please! Usher the ladies O-U-T!"

Harry doing his best. Half pushing, half cajoling them manages to ease them out *leaving with them, which is no easy task!*... "Goodnight Nate sleep tight. We'll see you in the morning at first light for our Sunrise ceremony, with our Revised Plan!"

Natewith finality!... *"Nite-All!"*

They're still arguing noisily as they leave. He straightens his old but comforting blank roll and crawls in immediately going into a deep overdue and welcome Sleep.

The Grande Epiphany

The Day of *The Grande Epiphany!* Early Morning has arrived The Sunrise Club meets at Nate's Bench to greet the Sun. And put together their long awaited *Master Plan!*

Nate full of energy and his old revitalized self, *Jumps* up on his Park Bench...*Boldly announces* . "There is a tide in the affairs of men which taken at Flood leads on to Fortune!... Thanks to the Bard and Julius Caesar for that!... This is that Tide Troops!...... Aah the Sun!...... The Sun! The Glorious Sun! Am I glad to be able to welcome it this morning with my head still attached and my hat still upon it!"

Everyone happy and exuberant that their beloved leader is back now join in on the festivities...And Greet the Sun--- Which he proudly leads them in!

"But soft! What light through yon Fifth Ave. Smog does Break? It is the Sun! Welcome Sun!... NOW---It's Time to Picket; everyone!"

Nate boldly *Builds it to a Frenzy!*

"Time to kick off 'OUR PLAN.' *(Energetically)* With THE MOST DYNAMIC PROTEST MARCH EVER UNDERTAKEN!"

Everyone joining in now, " For, Peace! Jobs! Food! Shelter! for Our HOMELESS, our JOBLESS, our VETS and the DISABLED!"

Nate excitedly requesting, "We need your ideas!... Nan take notes!... Harry!....Kick it off !"

This is a new Harry , Harry the Dynamo, The Activist with a cause! "Sure Boss!... And I want you all to know I gave this a lot of thought during the night... First, We increase our forces by advertising our cause with signs and by utilizing the Social Media to recruit thousands of people to march with us! Recruiting thousands of ordinary folk, to get those Boots marching for The Plan!... Enlist *Armies* of street people, Veterans; homeless, and jobless, the disabled in wheelchairs, those long neglected by *government,* and *society* into our, 'Revised Plan.' Then Deploy them into the Streets, Protesting! Protesting! Blocking traffic on the Brooklyn Bridge, converging on Wall Street, can be some of our options, our goal! This is the way we Deliver Our Message of Peace; and Aid for the needy!"

Nate asks, "Harry just how do we do this?"

" I've come up with some other good ideas for disseminating 'Our Plan' to the World along with the rest of the Sunshine Club, these last few days and say for starters I can ask my friends on the street; Vets from Wars in Iraq, Afghanistan, Vietnam even. Who can pass the word along. A regular 'Street Grapevine, they'll get word out by mouth, signs, and gatherings throughout the City!"

Mary now busting with her ideas says, " I know Parents, and Spouses, Relatives and Friends from my old neighborhood, who lost loved ones who served in the Wars; Korean, Nam' and the Middle East and then 911!... My Mom'll help me to get in touch with'em! They're not afraid to speak up and write letters and do the Social Networking stuff too and will I'm sure!"

Nate asks Nan, "can you get Media coverage for us? I know you do have some friends in high places!"

"Never thought you'd ask! I'll do my best... and get in touch with Media people I know and contact Veterans organizations and pro-action groups to spread the word! Utilize *Social Action Networks*... Also very important; set up a Non-Profit Organization for donations! We'll need money, for food, travel and expenses!"

"I'm really getting excited now, the way this is taking off!" Nate proudly adds, " Thanks Troops!"

Everyone even some early morning *Bystanders* get caught up in their enthusiasm offering to help... And now *In the Moment* all explode into a tumultuous excited; "Hooray!... Yaaaay!...Yaaay!"

Nate proclaiming, *"Everyone!* We're witnessing the Birth of a Patriotic Movement, *here!...* I'll do my best to raise Funds too! For *(Dynamically.)* 'THE PLAN!' 'OUR PLAN!" Hildy and Mayor, Will you join us in *This?"*

Hildy agrees to with a slight reservation, "I'll do everything I can, as long as it's *politically correct!"*

The Mayor adds his "Ditto!"… Everyone enjoying a good laugh that helps ease all tensions, then applaud till their hands hurt even a cop on the beat wondering what the commotion was all about and himself a Vet joins in along with a buddy!

"This is exploding right before our eyes!" Nate proudly exclaiming, "Great! Everyone knows what to do so let's do it! Boot up the *Social Action Networking,* get volunteers out Marching, Moving on in Wheelchairs, on Bikes. *Demand Legislation* be passed to Aid the Homeless, the Vets, the Disabled with Shelter, Food, Job Retraining so they can support themselves and families… In a World at Peace! Shouting our message from Street Corners, Sidewalks, The Web! For people in need in the USA! With our *Signs*, *Voices, Protesting, Votes and the Social Media!...* Our Mantras! Ringing in everyone's ears. *That's* our Goal! We'll March! Protest! March! Demand! Till we get *Action* ! ACTION! And Legislation to get us on our feet! We'll be a Starburst across the Skies of the U.S. for all the World to see! *They* All join in with their energetic, agitated, repetitive *incantations and Mantras…* Yay! Yay! Down with the Greedy… Jobs and Care for the Needy! We're sick and tired of WAR and not going to take it anymore! And finally blast out with *"Peace! Peace! Let All War Cease! May Jobs, Food, Shelter for all Homeless and Vets, Disabled, and Addicted Increase!"* Over and over! Till their voices were heard with one more **Big Shout Out!**

Look Out World here we Come!

Epilogue-

People passersby, those on the way to work, stopping, joining in offering to help... Signing up in the early morning, and later on the street corners, parks, even Wall Street and the NYC Bridges...Till We the People are heard and get results!

In the background we hear! The Mantra incanting: Peace!

Peace! Let All War Cease!'

'Down with War! It's pandemonium! Let freedom ring! Stop War-ring!'

' Jobs, Food, Shelter for the Homeless and Vet you Bet!' 'We're irate, War is not our fate!... End War before it's too late!' 'Down with the Greedy... Jobs and Care for the Needy!' Then at the top of their lungs! 'We're sick and tired of WAR and not going to take it anymore!')

THE END! ****** BUT A NEW BEGINNING!

About the Author

NICHOLAS CONTI- DGA--- Born in the shadow of the
Verrazano Bridge, Brooklyn; educated at St. John's Univ., &
CUNY in Communications. Served U.S. Navy 4 yrs, traveling
widely. Attended The American Academy of Dramatic Arts,
American Theater Wing,& Announcer Training Studios, NYC.
Studied Voice, Acting, Music privately. And have had 20 yrs.
as a Professional, Actor/Singer/ Radio/Announcer& member of
AEA, SAG, AGMA, AFTRA. *** A Playwright for 18 yrs. with
21 published plays/5 Publishers. In Nov. 2005 won an award at
Gettysburg College for their One Act Play Festival, with
performances and Honorarium, for "The Merry Women of
Windham," later published by Lazy Bee Scripts, UK...
Recently achieving 2nd place in the Confined Div., in the
Dundrum One Act Play Festival, Oct./Nov. 2009, Dublin
Ireland; performed by The Trinity Drama Group... And was
commissioned by the City of Poughkeepsie, NY, to write their
Historic Pageant, for the Quadricentennial, presented in May
2009. Feb 2013: Historical Fiction Published on
Amazon/Create Space and on Kindle: Titled: "Fables of the
Hudson Valley Miniscules." And in March 2013: A collection
of Hysterical, Topical, Medicinal, Loving, Adventurous,
somewhat Biographical, "PrimeTime Rhymes," joined by
"Jailhouse Armageddon,' or how to break into and out of a
Maximum State Prison; later by "The Cryacula Genesis." A
Frozen Horror Tale with a Bite! All on Amazon/CreateSpace.
And Kindle............. Thank You!... *Nicholas Conti* DGA

Nicholas Conti

www.ingramcontent.com/pod-product-compliance
Lightning Source LLC
Chambersburg PA
CBHW060401290526
45791CB00002B/577